T0248529

Praise for
The Babylon Bee Guide to the Apocalypse

"I'm definitely buying *The Babylon Bee's Guide to the Apocalypse*. Everyone should be prepared. CLIMATE CHANGE IS REAL! I think it's safe to say that a consensus of scientists believes that within 500 million years, the sun will heat up to such an extent that the earth will be uninhabitable. No time to waste. Forget the bunker, just begin sending methane-eating, oxygen-producing bacteria to Titan—now. That's my plan and I'm sticking to it."
  —Senator Rand Paul

"Forget food, shelter, and toilet paper! *The Babylon Bee Guide to the Apocalypse* is all you need to survive the end of the world. (Plus, it could probably double as food, shelter, and toilet paper.)"
  —Glenn Beck, New York Times best-selling author and nationally syndicated radio host

"More irreverent, offensive, and highly funny satire from my friends at The Bee. WARNING: while you might lose some brain cells, you will laugh out loud."
  —Dave Ramsey, bestselling author and radio host

"The End is Nigh!' And based on what I'm seeing, I can't wait! I've already meal-prepped for the apocalypse and charged my electric bike to make a beeline for the Mexican border where I intend to cross illegally and spend my Fallout days living in sin with Greta Thunberg, sipping iodide cocktails in the radiating desert sands, screaming 'WE TOLD YOU SO!' You better have a plan for the Big Bang, and this book can help you do it!"
  —Chad Prather, host of *The Chad Prather Show*

"Between climate change, lab-grown super viruses, AI deepfakes and Ivy League marxists in keffiyehs and ze/zir pronoun pins, you know the end is near. This handy guide covers everything you'll need to prepare, survive, and rebuild civilization from the ashes!"

—**Kelley Paul,** married to some guy named Rand

"This funny and accurate book from The Babylon Bee will help you survive the end of the world. And I should know a thing or two about survival. I was Hercules, Captain Dylan Hunt, and Kull the Conqueror. I was even Rayford Steele in *Left Behind*. Man, come to think of it, I should have written the book!"

—**Kevin Sorbo,** actor, producer, director, and speaker

"The Babylon Bee is what *Saturday Night Live* used to be when it was funny."

—**Larry Elder,** governor of California, in an alternate dimension

"The humor of The Babylon Bee left me enraptured, but will leave you in stitches."

—**Michael Malice,** author of *The White Pill*

"If you've ever wondered how the world will end and when, this book won't answer any of your questions. That's one of its principal virtues. Another is that it's hilarious. If you only have room in your survival kit for essential first-aid supplies or this book, choose this book. The bandages won't help anyway, and you might as well have a laugh about it."

—**Spencer Klavan,** writer and podcaster

"When you think of bad a****!!! fearless warriors !!!! few names come to mind…oh…read this book The Babylon Bee's new book is like the killer bees to the social justice woke mob…just take out the killer part and obviously they're not real bees…or even intimidating…kinda on the puny side…BUT !!! these guys are cool…as can be…given the…well enjoy the book…#nuffsaid"

—**Tyrus,** host of *Maintaining With Tyrus* on Outkick, Fox News contributor, NYT best-selling author, professional wrestler *(only the swear was adjusted, endorsement left as received)*

"I was already ready for the end of the world, and since reading *The Babylon Bee Guide to the Apocalypse*, I am readier. Or perhaps not, but it was fun."

    —Zuby, rapper, author, host of *Real Talk with Zuby* podcast

"What on earth is wrong with you??"

    —Beth Moore, American evangelist and author

"I told you guys to stop emailing me. How'd you even get my email in the first place?"

    —Joe Rogan, host of *The Joe Rogan Experience*

"This is a great book, and you should buy enough copies to sell through our advance."

    —Seth Dillon, owner and CEO of The Babylon Bee

"I am proud to endorse this book."

    —Travis Woodside, paid employee of The Babylon Bee

The Babylon Bee Guide to the Apocalypse

The Babylon Bee Guide to

THE APOCALYPSE

How to Survive All of the Possible World-Ending Scenarios, From Artificial Intelligence to Zombies

Since 1947
REGNERY

An Imprint of Skyhorse Publishing, Inc.

Copyright © 2024 by The Babylon Bee. This work is published by Regnery Publishing, through special arrangement with Salem Media Group. Regnery titles are distributed exclusively by Skyhorse Publishing, Inc.

All rights reserved. No part of this book may be reproduced in any manner without the express written consent of the publisher, except in the case of brief excerpts in critical reviews or articles. All inquiries should be addressed to Regnery, 307 West 36th Street, 11th Floor, New York, NY 10018.

Regnery books may be purchased in bulk at special discounts for sales promotion, corporate gifts, fund-raising, or educational purposes. Special editions can also be created to specifications. For details, contact the Special Sales Department, Regnery, 307 West 36th Street, 11th Floor, New York, NY 10018 or info@skyhorsepublishing.com.

Regnery is an imprint of Skyhorse Publishing, Inc.®, a Delaware corporation.

Visit our website at www.regnery.com.

Please follow our publisher Tony Lyons on Instagram @tonylyonsisuncertain.

10 9 8 7 6 5 4 3 2 1

Library of Congress Cataloging-in-Publication Data is available on file.

Print ISBN: 978-1-5107-8154-2
Ebook ISBN: 978-1-5107-8157-3

Printed in China

This book is dedicated to
the politicians in Washington, D.C.
who brought about the end of Western civilization
and made it possible for us to write this book
and capitalize on the end of the world.

Thank you.

CONTENTS

Introduction

Civilization Has Collapsed:
Are You Prepared?

It has finally happened. America has fallen. The world is in chaos. There's no question that we're about to be plunged into a period of tribulation, war, and a desperate struggle for survival.

Now the only question is: Will YOU be one of the survivors??

If you're reading this book, it's too late to stop the end of the world. But it's not too late to learn how to survive it—in style. In this handy guide, we draw on at least several hours of exhaustive research by The Babylon Bee's trusted journalists to show you how to survive any type of apocalypse, from zombies to armageddon and back again. So find yourself a hidey-hole, hunker down for a while, cook up some delicious cockroach meat, and start reading.

In this book, you'll learn how to fend for yourself, live off the land, and make lots of useful weapons that will help you fight off your enemies and look cool while doing it.

Here's just a small sampling of what this book includes:

WHAT'S IN THIS BOOK?

Handy fight moves

Recipes from common items you can find across the post-apocalyptic landscape

A comprehensive description of every possible apocalyptic scenario that could be unleashed on our world

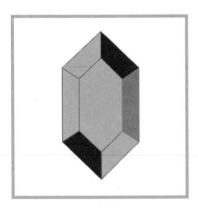

Currencies you should start hoarding now

Incredible business opportunities that are definitely not pyramid schemes

Beautiful illustrations

By the end of this book, you'll definitely be prepared for anything Armageddon can throw your way.

But let's back up and start at the beginning:

SIGNS THE END HAS COME

Not sure if the apocalypse is happening? That's odd. It's usually pretty obvious. But here are some things to look for:

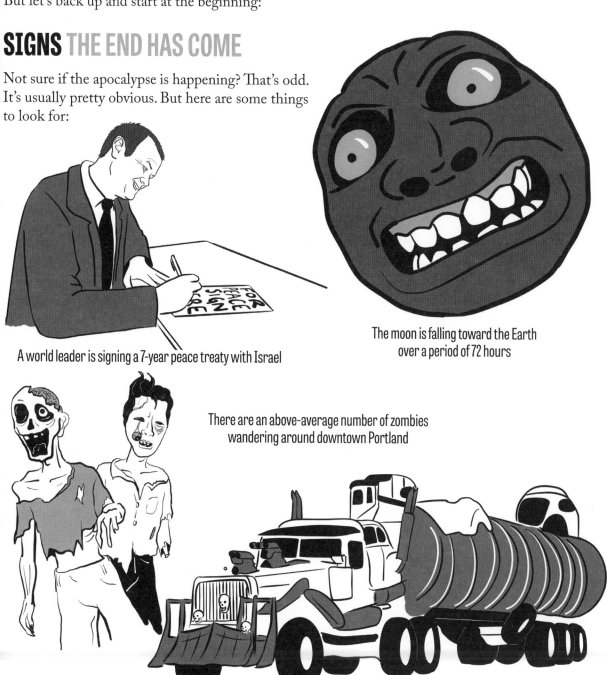

A world leader is signing a 7-year peace treaty with Israel

The moon is falling toward the Earth over a period of 72 hours

There are an above-average number of zombies wandering around downtown Portland

Tom Hardy is driving toward you in a war rig

SIGNS THE END HAS COME (CONTINUED)

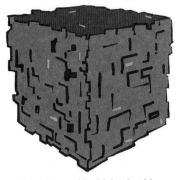

There's a cool-lookin' cube thing hovering above the Earth

Kirk Cameron is slowly floating into the sky

Over 17 mushroom clouds on the horizon

There is a communist flag flying over the White House

The work fridge is out of La Croix

Taco Bell has just announced a new Quadruple Cheesy Extra Beef Flamin' Hot Double-Decker Chalupa

TYPES OF APOCALYPSES YOU MAY ENCOUNTER (INEXHAUSTIVE)

Here are just a few of the possible ends of the world you might encounter:

Environmental Disasters

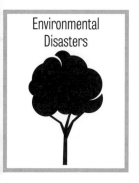

Exploding Death Virus

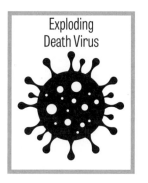

Nuclear Winter

Capitalistic Greed

Zombies

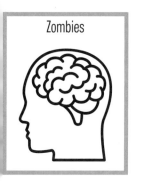

Communist Takeover

Mass Death by Robot

Net Neutrality

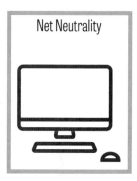

Emotional

Metaphorical
(the world can still end in your heart)

Bone-Type

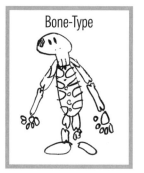

Other

If your particular apocalypse isn't covered here, don't worry. We'll cover lots more in the rest of the book.

But if you finish the whole thing, and we still haven't covered your apocalypse, well...you'll probably have to wait for the sequel. Which won't come. Because we'll likely all be dead.

HOW DO WE KNOW SO MUCH ABOUT THE APOCALYPSE, ANYWAY?

You might be wondering how we know all this great information about all the possible ends of the world. We actually built a trans-dimensional travel machine using spare parts we found around the office and a $12 crystal from a Hobby Lobby clearance shelf. Then, WE SENT BABYLON BEE EMPLOYEE TRAVIS into thousands of different universes to find out how they all end. Any time you see a TRAVIS' AVLOGALYPSE call-out box throughout the text, you're about to be treated to something very special: words from Travis' own mouth about how the world might end.

If you're committed and ready—mind, body, and soul—you can survive the apocalypse with our help. If you're ready, shout with us now to the skies: "I! AM! READY!"

Now get ready for us to learn ya' these great skills and more:

BASIC COMBAT MOVES

We'll cover more advanced fight moves later. But you should know the basics before you get ganked by some wasteland raiders right away.

Punch
Extend arm quickly with fingers curled into a ball shape.

Kick
Extend foot quickly with toes pointed. Helps if you make a grunting noise.

HOW TO SCAVENGE FOR FOOD

Surviving isn't just about killing opposing warlords and fighting off hordes of space aliens—though that's most of it.

It's also important for you to know how to keep yourself sustained with delicious, mostly edible food. And there ain't DoorDash after the apocalypse, so you'll need to learn these food scavenging skills if you have any hope of making it until we rebuild society:

Brewing delicious craft beer out of irradiated water and fermented tumbleweeds

Rummaging for old bags of Takis in abandoned grocery stores

Cooking squirrel sous vide for a classy meal

Learning to appreciate the taste of old car tires

COBBLE TOGETHER COOL SURVIVAL TOOLS

Everyone likes weapons, but tools are just as important as weapons. You might say that tools are just weapons for your problems. This book will show you how to make a bunch of cool survival tools from items commonly found in an apocalyptic wasteland.

Here are a few examples:

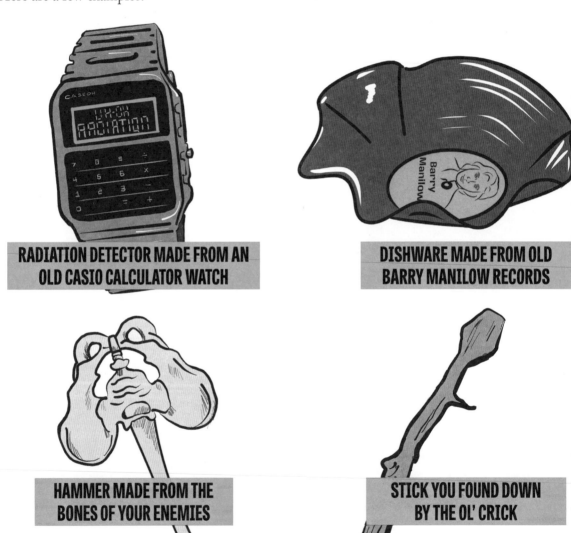

RADIATION DETECTOR MADE FROM AN OLD CASIO CALCULATOR WATCH

DISHWARE MADE FROM OLD BARRY MANILOW RECORDS

HAMMER MADE FROM THE BONES OF YOUR ENEMIES

STICK YOU FOUND DOWN BY THE OL' CRICK

THE COOLEST WAYS TO DIE

Sometimes, you just have to admit it's the end. You're surrounded by zombies, flesh-eating hordes of aliens from the dark side of Pluto, or angry Tesla robots controlled by malevolent AI, and you've just gotta decide to throw in the towel and go out in a blaze of glory.

In this book, we'll teach you how to die the most epic end-of-the-world deaths possible:

Shouting "Go on without me!" as the rest of your team escapes in a truck and you mow down thousands of zombies before finally succumbing to your wounds

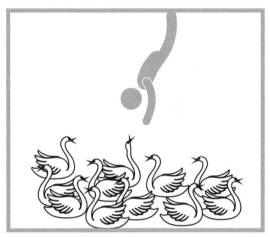

Epic swan dive into horde of mutant swans

Challenging the AI robot boss to one-on-one-combat

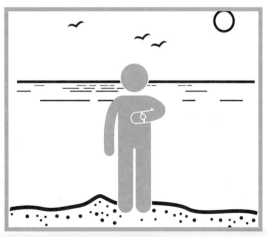

Slowly roasting alive as the global temperatures rise by 1 degree each year

HOW TO ASSEMBLE THE PERFECT APOCALYPSE SURVIVAL TEAM

One of the most important factors in whether or not you'll survive the apocalypse is who your teammates are. There is no "I" in "post-apocalypse dream team," after all.

So, for the purposes of this exercise, you've saved up $12,000 and can recruit as many people as you want listed in the table below to your apocalypse survival squad. Who you goin' with?

BUILD YOUR SURVIVAL TEAM FOR $12,000

$13,000	Kyle Rittenhouse				
$5,000	Mad Max	Reacher	Kirk Cameron	Your crazy MAGA neighbor with tons of guns	The Master Chief
$4,000	Kevin Sorbo	*Portal* turret	Cortana (from *Halo*)	The cast of the 1983 production of *The Pirates of Penzance*	Link
$3,000	Three monkeys stacked up in a trench coat	Grimace	Elon Musk	A resourceful hobo from the smallest town	Prison Mike
$2,000	Coco Crisp (Former Oakland Athletic)	Mark Zuckerberg	Angry Karen	Newt Gingrich	Steve
$1,000	Cocoa Crisp (knockoff breakfast cereal)	A man with an accordion	Cortana (From Microsoft Windows)	A woman with one leg	A fun talking animal companion for comic relief

BUILD YOUR OWN APOCALYPSE

Perhaps you are reading this book pre-apocalypse, so you don't know what type of threats you may need to prepare for. In such cases, you simply need to be prepared for any and every possible disaster situation. Use the following generator to produce a randomized apocalypse scenario, then write a 30-page essay detailing survival tactics for that particular apocalypse.

Pick your favorite five-letter word (no cuss words, please):

Your apocalypse is a/an:

Example using: D-E-A-T-H=
YOUR APOCALYPSE IS A
Crimson Island Ravaged by
Mathematically Challenged Beverages

RANDOMIZED APOCALYPSE SCENARIO GENERATOR

A. Desert	A. Hellscape	A. Ravaged by	A. Zombie	A. Monkeys
B. Dusty	B. Wasteland	B. Overrun with	B. Mysterious	B. Disease
C. Feral	C. Planet	C. Brimming with	C. Legendary	C. Mutant sharks
D. Crimson	D. Dystopia	D. Governed by	D. Malevolent	D. Locusts
E. Toasty	E. Island	E. With the essence of	E. Demon	E. Horsefolk
F. Uninhabitable	F. Realm	F. Known for its	F. Finely crafted	F. Bud Light
G. Torrential	G. Ecosphere	G. With a side of	G. Golden	G. Space Amoeba
H. Socially awkward	H. Office party	H. With an absence of	H. Alcoholic	H. Beverages
I. Inept	I. Flat Earth	I. Where people worship	I. Gentle	I. Robots
J. Thirsty	J. Cavern	J. Hosting	J. Foolish	J. Moonmen
K. Sinful	K. Iceberg	K. In the shape of	K. Infected	K. Praying Mantises
L. Robotic	L. Day care	L. Lightly flavored by	L. Feisty	L. Democrats
M. Intelligent	M. Galaxy	M. Unassociated with	M. Enraged	M. Tampons
N. Unsatisfactory	N. Cryochamber	N. Chock full of	N. Homosexual	N. Homosexuals
O. Emasculated	O. Biosphere	O. With a penchant for	O. Acid-breath	O. Travis clones
P. Vaporized	P. Volcano	P. With a distaste for	P. Monochromatic	P. Cults
Q. Submerged	Q. Cottage	Q. Smothered with	Q. Cannibalistic	Q. Ulcers
R. Wonderful	R. Continent	R. Ruled by the Legion of	R. Unshowered	R. Legions
S. Decimated	S. Tundra	S. Which welcomes	S. Shifty	S. Chinese spies
T. Underrated	T. Anarchist state	T. With a citizenry of	T. Mathematically challenged	T. Werewolves
U. Lava-covered	U. Warzone	U. Judged by	U. Beautiful	U. Republicans
V. Rookie	V. Place	V. Governed by	V. Racist	V. Miners
W. Evil	W. Free-for-all	W. Whose currency is	W. Based	W. Libertarians
X. Dragon-filled	X. Apartment	X. Harboring	X. Voluptuous	X. Frogmen
Y. Decrepit	Y. Nation-state	Y. On the take from	Y. Slimy	Y. Carrots
Z. Decaying	Z. Society	Z. With ill-gotten	Z. Slippery	Z. Cordyceps

WHAT VIDEO GAMES CAN TEACH US ABOUT SURVIVAL

One of the most important ways to train for the end of the world is to boot up the trusty ol' video game console and play some vidyagames. Here are a few helpful lessons...

Avoid pointy death spikes

Save all your health potions
for the final boss

Climbable ledges are clearly
marked with white or
yellow paint

Crafting tools and weapons is
as easy as slapping a couple
ingredients together

If you're losing,
you can just log off

Don't forget to quicksave before
you face a tough enemy

Headshots are worth more

Cut grass to find currency

The gyroids in *Animal Crossing*
are sentient

THIS IS THE END OF THE CHAPTER—AND THE WORLD—

BUT IT'S JUST THE BEGINNING OF THIS BOOK

We hope this short introduction has gotten you pumped up about the end of the world. We sure are. Because we're prepared.

Now join us on this epic journey to get

PREPPED,

LOCKED,

and

LOADED

for the end of the world.

Are you ready?

TRAVIS' A VLOG ALYPSE

INSTRUCTIONS

As we sent Travis to the multiverse of apocalyptic scenarios, he was kind enough to record VLOGs updating us on what's going on in each of those universes.

Whenever you see one of these QR codes, scan it with your smartphone to catch a glimpse into Travis' crazy trip through all possible ends of the world. If the internet no longer exists, well, then, you have bigger problems, don't you?

https://babylonbee.com/books/
apocalypse/instructions

Chapter 1

Building an Awesome Survival Bunker

The most important aspect of surviving in any scenario is staying alive. If you don't stay alive, one could argue that you're not really surviving at all.

The most important element to surviving whatever the end times has to throw at you is having an impenetrable bunker. Every superhero has his base of operations: Superman has the Fortress of Solitude, Batman has the Batcave, and Donald Trump has Mar-a-Lago.

And now it's your turn. Join us as we give you all the best tips on how to get started making your very own survival bunker to help you outlast all those other chumps.

SO YOU WANNA BUILD A BUNKER?

Bunker owners get a bad rap. In normal times, bunker owners are often viewed as crazy, paranoid, anti-social, and, quite frankly, ugly. But when disaster strikes, everyone suddenly praises the bunker crazies as being wise and full of foresight. In the midst of disaster, many people will attempt to cozy up to bunker owners. However, these bunker owners have long since eschewed any normal relationships and will usually shoot anyone trying to approach and ask for shelter on sight.

The moral of the story? Build your own bunker before it's too late.

WHERE DO I BUILD MY BUNKER?

Here are a few ideal locations for your very first survival bunker:

PRETTY MUCH ANYWHERE IN MONTANA

THE ABANDONED STARCOURT MALL

AN OLD CASTLE

OLD MISSILE SILO

UNDER THE TALLEST TREE IN THE FOREST

ON THE FLOATING ISLAND OF TRASH IN THE PACIFIC OCEAN

300 FEET UNDERGROUND

DIGGING A BUNKER

Unless you happen to own an abandoned missile silo, building a proper bunker will most likely require a lot of digging. Although construction vehicles exist for large-scale building projects, it's probably best to utilize tools that will not draw unwanted attention from the feds. For that reason, **WE STRONGLY RECOMMEND USING A SHOVEL.**

BUNKER DEFENSE

One of the most important parts of any bunker is defending it. Make sure your survival abode is ready for any kind of assault with these fun and useful additions:

BUNKER DEFENSE TD

1. *Home Alone* traps
2. A simple mummy's curse
3. Falling rocks
4. A video game kiosk outside your bunker that plays a never-ending game of Mario Party so that any potential invaders get distracted forever playing Mario Party until they are dead.[1]
5. A sassy ghost
6. Caltrops
7. 3 pitbulls taped together to create the ultimate weapon
8. A moat filled with acid and piranhas
9. Pizza cannon
10. Razor wire

[1] The worst part is that they lose all their stars at the end.

BAD GUYS START HERE

STOCKING YOUR BUNKER

A hole in the ground will protect you from a myriad of nightmare circumstances, but much like a person, it's what's on the inside that really counts.

As the hobo who lives outside our office always says, "You might survive the blast, but how long can you last?" If your bunker is not properly equipped, the answer to that question very well may be, "Not that long, Hobo Hank!" (And his name's not even Hank). Here are some bunker essentials and how you can use them to extend your life and cheat death itself:

CHICK-FIL-A STOCKPILE
You want to stockpile a lot of Chick-fil-A, because they're closed on Sunday, and you'll inevitably crave it on Sunday. Also, all the Chick-fil-A's will be exploded in a nuclear fire, most likely.

BIBLE
KJV only, please.

WEIGHTED COMPANION CUBE
Equal parts lovable and useful. A friend through good times and bad.

STANLEY CUPS
You'll need something to drink out of during the apocalypse, and you won't live down the embarrassment if you have a lame Yeti cup.

THE SAME OLD PAIR OF ROLLER BLADES YOU'VE HAD SINCE 1998
Never know when you're gonna use them again.

COPY OF BBC'S 1995 ADAPTATION OF *PRIDE & PREJUDICE* ON VHS
Entertainment is essential if you don't want to go crazy and kill each other as you wait for the radiation to die down, and there's no better way to whittle away the time than by getting lost in the complex social web woven by Elizabeth and Mr. Darcy. Just don't accidentally stock up on the 2005 film version, or you'll go crazy even faster. Psh...Keira Knightley.

BUCKETS OF PATRIOTIC-BRANDED SURVIVAL FOOD
They may laugh at your America First Patriot USA Red White & Blue food buckets now, but they won't be laughing when you're getting 2000 calories a day, and they're scavenging for squirrel meat.

COOL SWORD
Good for looking cool in front of your friends and also defense.

COPY OF DC TALK'S *JESUS FREAK* ON VINYL
You will listen to it every single day, and you will not go crazy. Probably. Also, you'll be preserving important art for future generations.

AXIS & ALLIES: ANNIVERSARY EDITION
You'll have so much time to play board games! What better way to spend your time during World War III than by simulating World War II over and over again?

CROSSWORD PUZZLE
These are great for passing the time. Don't have one? TURN TO THE NEXT PAGE. Crossword puzzle books can cost over $7 on Amazon, but we'll give you one for free.

BITCOIN WALLET
When you finally get out of the bunker, you'll be the richest (and possibly only) person alive!

TOMATO SEEDS
You'll surely be ready for the apocalypse if you can painstakingly grow a few tomatoes with several months of grueling work.

FREE CROSSWORD PUZZLE (MSRP $6.99)

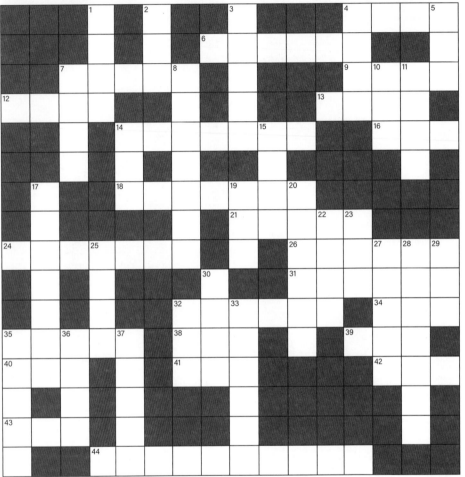

DOWN

1 *Growing Pains* star
2 Kentucky ark enthusia
3 Hebrew critical rappe
4 "Hey! Listen!"
5 Elizabeth Warren's greeting
7 A fool, according to Gandalf
8 The flattest breakfast
10 Dope, sick, etc.
11 EV Tycoon
14 EVs don't need this
15 Developer of *Diddy Kong Racing*
17 Largest object known to man (2 words)
19 Paper marker
20 Affluent "minister"
22 Given to Jan 6 protestors by Capitol Police
23 Don't call GameStop transgenders this
25 An action word
27 Not a winner
28 Didn't kill himself
29 Golf stand
30 Interstellar spice franchise
32 Singing tomato
33 SF's hypodermic decoration
35 Not the size of Trump's hands
36 Roaches' bane
37 Negotiation starter

ACROSS

4 OG Ark Enthusiast
6 Cackling VP
7 The one true president
9 *The* ___ with Whoopi
12 Harder to get than a gun, according to Obama
13 Saxophone president
14 There are only two
16 Had a salty wife
18 Hebraic chart-topping rapper
21 Bird shelters
24 To continue living

26 SF sidewalk
31 Continent comprised of a bunch of silly countries
32 Fortified shelter
34 Opposite of NNW
35 Herculean talent
38 Number of Gods
39 Rock or other domesticated companion
40 Gina Carano's sport
41 Babylonian winged insect
42 Communist color
43 One who loves berries and cream
44 1998 Bruce Willis film

LET'S SPRUCE THINGS UP!

Now that you have your very own bunker, you may have noticed that it's still lacking some pizzazz. The bare concrete look might be in right now, but that doesn't mean you have to live like some sort of degenerate New York postmodern artist. Here are some proven design tips to bring a little more life and sunshine (or sunshine-like light sources) to your bunker.

Ferns

Who doesn't like ferns? Every house should have ferns, so why not every bunker too?

Wall Stickers That Look Like Windows

You can get these on Amazon for pretty cheap. When seen from the corner of your eye, they may allow you to forget for a split second that you're buried underground, and that your old life has been obliterated along with every major US city.

Swords

This goes without saying, but swords are common staples of every and any design aesthetic, so why should bunker design be any different? The type of sword or swords you choose to display can communicate a lot about who you are as a person. Broadswords show strength and boldness in both character and action. Katanas signal that you are able to focus on specific goals in your life and make them happen. Movie replica swords show an appreciation for the arts and also your willingness (some might even say eagerness) to part with monetary riches to purchase a facsimile of a movie prop. But you do you, I guess.

Streamers

Crepe paper streamers are a cost-effective way to make it seem like a party every day! You don't have to save them for birthdays when they can add so much brightness and cheer to any occasion. You can purchase an 81ft long roll from Party City for only a dollar, although they also come in a single-colored 6-pack for $7.99. We're not sure why the 6-pack would actually end up costing more than the individual ones, plus if you get them individually you could choose more colors. We'll have to ask the manager if that pricing is right cause it'd be weird if that's the right price.

Paint

It may sound simple, but painting a room a new color will not only change your feelings about the room, but can also uplift your overall mood and emotional health. A vibrant red can stimulate your appetite, increase blood flow, and trigger a blood rage to increase your fighting power against potential intruders. A bright yellow is reminiscent of warm sunlight, the comfort of melting butter on bread, or it can also remind you that the threat of the Communist Chinese Party that started all this nonsense in the first place is still present and you need to be ready to fight back when the right day comes. Yellow, because of their skin color.

LET'S SPRUCE THINGS UP! (CONTINUED)

Chalk Paint

Chalk paint is an excellent way of sprucing up salvaged pieces of furniture. You'll be doing a lot of salvaging, so we highly recommend utilizing chalk paint to turn your otherwise shabby furniture into shabby chic. Pair it with a few fine-grain sanding sponges to give your dresser a lovingly used look that remains timeless and integrates well into almost any design aesthetic.

A Single Thomas Kinkade Painting

Are you a Christian with a penchant for dreamy lighting in oil paintings? Look no further. Exercise caution so as not to purchase any Chinese counterfeits. They are valueless fakes and also communist, but I repeat myself.

Throw Pillows

If there's any small bit of knowledge mankind has wrested from the mysterious minds of women, it is that they derive their energy by maintaining a close proximity to throw pillows. No one knows why, no one knows how, however, it is evident from the overflowing mounds of throw pillows on every woman's couch or bed that there surely must be a utilitarian purpose for such obsessive and costly monuments of fluff.

Shiplap

Ever want to feel like you're on a ship, but you don't want to go through the hassle of actually boarding a ship like some sort of peasant? Introducing: Shiplap. Made with reclaimed wood, refinished, and varnished with pumpkin spice. Order in the next 5 minutes and your planks will be personally blessed by Joanna Gaines herself.

TRAVIS' A VLOG ALYPSE
SHELTER

Scan the QR code
to access a special bonus
video feed Travis doesn't
know about! Tee-hee!

https://babylonbee.com/books/
apocalypse/shelter

BUNKER RULES

It's important to set rules for your bunker. All guests of your bunker must follow your bunker rules and put the toilet paper on the OBJECTIVELY CORRECT way, Steve. Not all bunkers will have the same rules so this list of rules can be customized to your specific preferences. Better yet, grab a friend and ask them for the details to fill in without telling them the context of the rules.

THESE ARE THE RULES OF
THE _____ BUNKER OF _____
[ADJECTIVE]   [YOUR NAME HERE]

1. There shall be no _____ allowed on the premises. Anyone caught violating this rule will be sentenced to
   [PLURAL NOUN]
   a/an _____ death from a thousand _____ _____.
   [ADJECTIVE]   [ADJECTIVE]   [PLURAL NOUN]

2. On the 5th day of each month, all bunker dwellers must procure a _____ to be offered in a ceremony of
   [NOUN]
   remembrance of Earth's passing.

3. On each Wednesday, all bunker inhabitants must participate in the community potluck. Dishes must never contain
   _____, 'cause that would make the food all _____ and nobody wants that, Steve.
   [INGREDIENT]   [ADJECTIVE]

4. If you win the annual _____ tournament, you shall have a golden _____ placed upon your
   [GAME]   [OBJECT]
   head, and all bunker citizens must address you by your earned title of _____ _____ for
   [ADJECTIVE]   [TITLE OF A PERSON]
   a period of 3 months. Your food allowance will also be increased by one extra _____ per meal while
   [NOUN]
   supplies last.

5. Toilet paper rolls must be replaced by whomever utilizes the final sheet of a given roll and must be replaced with
   the dispensing end oriented on the side opposite of the wall. Failure to comply with this rule will result in immediate
   expulsion from the bunker and/or public execution. This rule is universal and cannot be altered to fit personal
   preference, as fallacious opinions are rendered invalid in this realm of objective truth and morality.

6. _____ is NOT ALLOWED in the bunker anymore. Not after the incident with the _____.
   [NAME OF PERSON]   [PLURAL NOUN]
   That was wild.

7. After the hours of _____ o' clock, all _____ must be silenced to prevent drawing unwanted attention
   [NUMBER]   [PLURAL NOUN]
   from the wandering hordes of _____ _____ shambling above our heads.
   [ADJECTIVE]   [PLURAL NOUN]

FOOD

Everybody needs to eat. Except for robots. But even they need to eat electricity and batteries and oil and...like...computer chips or something. So yeah, everybody needs to eat. In many apocalypse scenarios, food is a scarce commodity. Grocery stores may shut down, farms burnt or otherwise decimated, and drinking water contaminated. Over the next several pages, we will cover various methods of scrounging for food, determining the safety of potential food sources, and what unconventional foods you may need to resort to if you're in a pickle. Although if you're in a pickle, we suppose you could simply eat said pickle.

You know the basic food types, but which ones are best for survival?

FOODS YOU'LL NEED

SQUIRREL MEAT
+2 to sneakiness

CAT MEAT
+2 to night vision

IGUANA MEAT
+3 to branch clinging

HIPPO MEAT (RARE)
No stat bonus, just delicious

RICE AND BEANS
+5 budgeting skills

TWINKIES
+10 pounds

POWER PELLETS
+infinity ghost killing

SUPER MUSHROOM
Activates immediate growth spurt

PILLS!
It doesn't matter what kind, just eat em!

MIXED HERB (GREEN + YELLOW)
Restores a small amount of health and increases Leon's maximum health

DUBIOUS FOOD
Still heals you, but not as much. Gross!

STAMINA POTION
+4 stamina

Any food item's HP value doubles when cooked at an inn or in your personal dwelling.

INFERIOR SHELTER TYPES

- Tent
- Lean-to
- Treehouse
- Kiddie pool turned upside-down
- Cardboard fort
- Those weird hammock things that mountain climbers use. Scary!
- Repurposing a prison/hospital
- A house made out of goat flesh. Yum!
- Highway underpass
- Atop the tallest tree in the forest
- Sewer

INFERIOR SHELTER:
ATOP THE TALLEST TREE IN THE FOREST

TRAVIS' AVLOGALYPSE

TRAVIS' COOKING KORNER

Scan the QR code
to watch Travis
prepare a delicious
apocalypse meal.

https://babylonbee.com/books/
apocalypse/cooking

FOODS TO AVOID

Not all foods are worth pursuing. Some foods can have a deleterious effect on your health or just might taste gross and make you gag. Avoid these foods at all costs.

Human Flesh

It's a new world. You may be tempted to take a bite out of Steve. But before you do: DON'T.

Poison

Poison is bad for you. Try to avoid eating it in large quantities.

Funyuns

Just 'cause they're gross.

Irradiated Radroach Meat

Normal radroach meat is fine, just not the irradiated kind. Now that I think about it, I guess roaches only become radroaches when irradiated. Never mind. Just don't eat them.

The Blue Pill

Both the physical AND metaphorical kinds.

Suspicious sludge on the ground at the edge of your camp

Really good advice for before, during, OR after the apocalypse.

FOODS TO AVOID (CONTINUED)

Packet in your beef jerky that says "Silica Gel: DO NOT EAT"

It's really not as tasty as it looks. Not that we would know.

Yellow snow

Self-explanatory.

Non-patriotic food supplies

Don't get caught eating COMMUNIST food supplies. ONLY eat trusted sources of survival food buckets, such as those from MY PATRIOT SUPPLY, which you can buy NOW using promo code PREPAREWITHBEE for a great deal including free shipping on orders over $99. That's PREPAREWITHBEE.COM.

That weird green jello salad thing they make in Ohio

Ohio—can anything good come from there? No.

A mysterious green potion given to you by a wizard near the stream that meets a boulder in a distant wood

He may say it is for your own good. His claims are not as wonderful as they may sound.

Turkish Delight

It's a trap!

YOUR FINISHED BUNKER

After all that work, your bunker should look a little something like this:

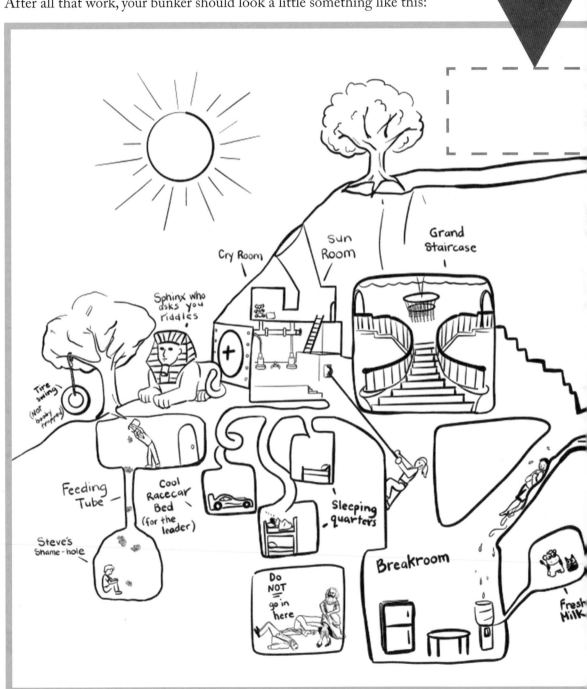

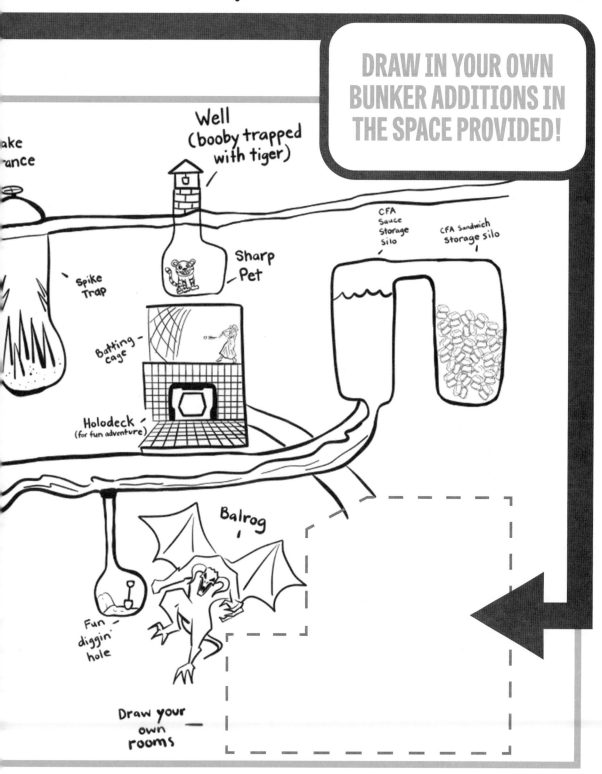

DRAW IN YOUR OWN BUNKER ADDITIONS IN THE SPACE PROVIDED!

Are you a conservative? Here are a few things especially for you to stock up on before the Apocalypse:

TOP 8 THINGS CONSERVATIVES SHOULD STOCK UP ON

Trump NFTs

There's a decent chance these will end up being treated as currency in the civilization to come.

Copies of all your political rants from social media so you can tell everyone "I told you so!"

Important.

The Art of the Deal

It's important to save the foundational works of Western civilization so we can rebuild society from the ashes.

Enough ammo to fend off billions of flesh-eating mutants

Just put it on your credit card.

Pre-censorship Dr. Seuss books

Remembering the way things once were will help you carry on.

Pogs

All of the other pogs in the world will be destroyed— just think of the fortune you'll make having the only ones.

COVID masks

To burn for warmth.

Donald Trump's DNA

President Clone Trump will help us rebuild the biggest, most beautiful society anyone has ever seen!

01 | BUILDING AN AWESOME SURVIVAL BUNKER
FIELD TRAINING EXERCISES

1. Would you rather be stuck in a bunker with Jar Jar Binks or Kreacher from Harry Potter?

   _____

2. If you were given a pack of Doritos, a Diet Dr. Pepper, and two goat hooves, what kind of dinner would you cook? There are no wrong answers.

   _____

3. While we have learned how to shelter our bodies in this chapter, the lingering problem remains that we must learn how to truly shelter our hearts. I guess that's not really a question, but more of an observation. You can ignore the following line.

   _____

4. When you're done decorating your bunker, do you think you could help me with mine? I dig your style.

   _____

Chapter 2

The
Climate Crisis

If you want to survive the apocalypse, you must be ready for the most terrifying world-ending scenario in human history:

~~global warming!~~
~~climate change!~~
THE CLIMATE EMERGENCY!

The climate emergency will kill us all. This is certain, according to 158% of the climate scientists we interviewed in our research for this guide.

As we were writing this guide, experts confirmed that "global warming" and "climate change" were outdated terms. "Climate Emergency" is the new, 100% scientific term approved by real scientists to make sure everyone is sufficiently frightened. EMERGENCY!"

If we do not act now to raise everyone's taxes and make everyone drive a battery-powered Subaru the earth will slowly warm over several centuries, causing warmer climates, which will cause the sea level to rise, which will lead to Barack Obama's house being underwater, which will lead to everyone dying of dehydration, or becoming a cannibal, or becoming a cannibal and then dying from dehydration. You don't want that to happen—just trust us on this.

This chapter will help you keep an eye out for signs of the climate apocalypse, give you pointers for how to stop it, and provide step-by-step instructions on how to survive once it happens.

HISTORY OF ~~GLOBAL WARMING~~ ~~CLIMATE CHANGE~~ THE CLIMATE EMERGENCY

The climate emergency was created in 1776, when a group of racist white men got together and decided to destroy the planet with capitalism. Their diabolical plot involved creating so much peace and human prosperity that the human population would grow and innovate, creating an industrial revolution that would provoke Mother Gaia and end in the total destruction of the Earth.

Over the years, many brave climate heroes fought back against the climate emergency by courageously reducing the human impact on the climate. Here are just a few:

THE HALL OF CLIMATE HEROES

1. **CAIN**
   Killed his brother Abel, who was a livestock farmer with a shameful carbon footprint.

2. **GENGHIS KHAN**
   His blood-soaked conquest of the planet reduced human impact by over 40 million people! Nice job, Genghis!

3. **HITLER**
   Human presence on the planet is...undesirable. Hitler understood this.

4. **STALIN**
   Scientists estimate he removed over 20 million people-worth of carbon from the atmosphere.

5. **MAO**
   The undisputed master of fighting climate change, Mao quadrupled the carbon-elimination of Stalin, and did a great job with public shaming events for people who resisted.

6. **XANDER**
   This antifa member from Portland only drinks fair-trade coffee and has vowed to never have kids. Way to go, Xander!

In order to be prepared for the worst, you must always keep an eye out for meteorological signs that the climate will soon rear its angry head and destroy the world. The signs are everywhere. Here are just a few signs that climatological destruction is right around the corner:

UNDENIABLE SIGNS OF THE CLIMATE APOCALYPSE

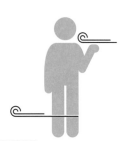

It is hot

If you go outside and it's a bit toasty, you can't deny it any longer: the climate is changing.

It is cold

If you go outside and it's a bit nippy, you can't deny it any longer: the climate is changing.

It is raining

Rain is absolute proof of climate change.

It is not raining

A lack of rain is absolute proof of climate change.

It's snowing

It literally never snowed before cars were invented. Climate change!

It's not snowing

It literally never did not not snow before cars were invented. Climate change!

NDENIABLE SIGNS OF THE CLIMATE APOCALYPSE (CONTINUED)

It's a pleasant day

A nice day outside? In Minnesota? CLIMATE. CHANGE.

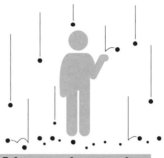

It's not a pleasant day

A not-so-nice day outside? In California? CLIMATE. CHANGE.

It is summer

When it's summer, it's hot, proving the climate is changing.

It is winter

When it's winter, it's cold, proving the climate is changing.

You feel sad

This is Mother Earth using the psychosphere to warn your chakra that you will soon be dead from the climate.

You feel happy, euphoric

This is the result of evil forces trying to lull you into a false sense of security so you won't fight climate change. DON'T LISTEN TO IT!

CAUSES OF THE CLIMATE APOCALYPSE

There are many causes of the climate apocalypse, but the main thing you should understand is that this is YOUR FAULT. Just look at you—breathing! Every breath secretes a deadly planet-killing poison called CO_2. And you're reading this book on paper, which likely came from a tree. That's two strikes already, pal.

Here's a list of things you should blame for your inevitable doom. Read them with anger in your heart until it bubbles over into a bubbling soup of rage.

- Gas-powered cars
- Electric cars
- Really, any form of transportation that gets a human being from point A to point B
- People eating food
- People drinking water
- People being alive for any reason whatsoever
- People not dying
- People not being communist
- Israel
- MAGA hats
- Children

MAGICAL ITEMS THAT DO NOT CAUSE CLIMATE CHANGE

Leonardo DiCaprio's super yacht
Studies show that it has a 0% chance of contributing to climate change, but a 100% chance of Leo standing on the prow shouting "I'm the king of the world!"

EV batteries
EV battery production lowers carbon emissions because the electricity comes from your house instead of the coal plant. It's science.

Private jet flights to events about climate change
If you are chartering a private jet in the pursuit of climate justice, the pollution doesn't really count. Al Gore says so, and he's never wrong.

Acorns
Acorns are largely inconsequential in relative terms to the larger discourse surrounding climate change.

HOW TO STOP THE CLIMATE APOCALYPSE

It might be too late to stop what's coming, but it doesn't hurt to try, and you'll gain a stellar reputation for being a noble and virtuous climate warrior—just like Stalin! If you want to give it your all and stop the inevitable disaster, try these scientifically proven methods of climate action:

STAND IN THE MIDDLE OF A BUSY HIGHWAY WITH YOUR FRIENDS AND SING SONGS

THROW FOOD AT EXPENSIVE ART

ONLY USE ELECTRIC APPLIANCES POWERED BY COAL

BECOME A MULTI-BILLIONAIRE, PURCHASE A PRIVATE JET AND FLY TO VARIOUS CLIMATE SUMMITS ALL AROUND THE WORLD AND GIVE SPEECHES

EAT SOY LENTIL PASTE INSTEAD OF STEAK

STOP HAVING CHILDREN

GLUE YOU AND YOUR FRIENDS TO CERTAIN THINGS

KILL PEOPLE

BAN HAIRSPRAY AND ONLY USE HAIR GEL

HOW TO STOP THE CLIMATE APOCALYPSE (CONTINUED)

VOTE FOR COMMUNISTS

REENGINEER THE ENTIRE WORLD ECONOMY AND 200 YEARS OF TECHNOLOGICAL INNOVATION TO STOP THE GLOBAL RELIANCE ON FOSSIL FUELS

BLOW UP THE SUN WITH A MISSILE

BAN PLASTIC UNTIL IT LEADS TO DEFORESTATION, THEN BAN PAPER UNTIL IT LEADS TO PLASTIC POLLUTION, THEN BAN PLASTIC AGAIN UNTIL IT LEADS TO DEFORESTATION, THEN BAN PAPER AGAIN UNTIL IT LEADS TO MORE PLASTIC POLLUTION

CREATE A RACE OF INTELLIGENT MACHINES, SCORCH THE SUN, SURRENDER YOUR BODY TO THE MATRIX TO BE USED FOR ENERGY

SUPPORT HAMAS, FOR SOME REASON

SAY A SILENT PRAYER TO THE SPIRIT OF AL GORE

CLAIM THE WORLD IS ENDING IN TEN YEARS; WAIT TEN YEARS; REPEAT

We encourage you to stop what you're doing immediately and do all of the things on this list right away. If only a small percentage of the five billion people who read this book follow these instructions, imagine what an impact you could make!

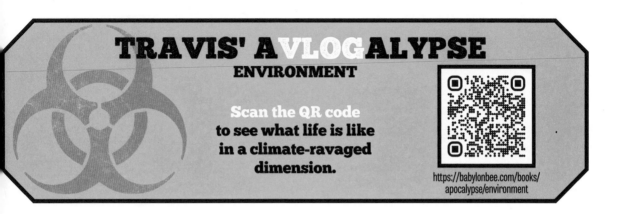

HOW TO SURVIVE THE CLIMATE APOCALYPSE

Now, we are finally at the most important section.

What follows is a complete guide to surviving the inevitable disaster that will soon befall us. Before we begin, it's important to know that you will not survive.

This will definitely kill you.

You should be absolutely terrified.

There is no hope whatsoever.

Even so, we experts at The Babylon Bee feel a duty to give you all the climate change survival tips we can to give you the best shot possible. Even though it won't work, and you'll die.

YOUR GEAR

Suit up, survivors!

Turn to the next page to see everything you will need to wear at all times in order to live through the climate emergency.

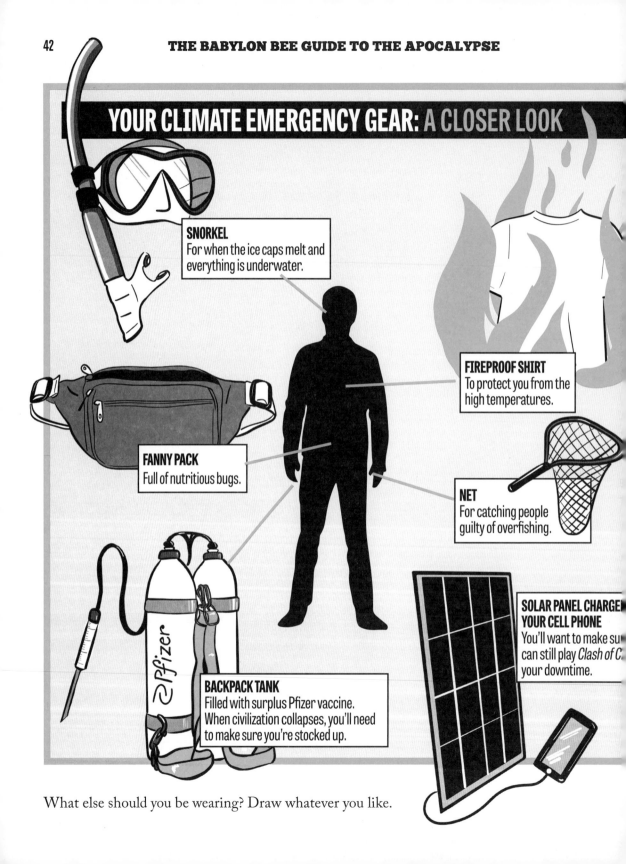

YOUR CLIMATE EMERGENCY GEAR: A CLOSER LOOK

SNORKEL
For when the ice caps melt and everything is underwater.

FIREPROOF SHIRT
To protect you from the high temperatures.

FANNY PACK
Full of nutritious bugs.

NET
For catching people guilty of overfishing.

BACKPACK TANK
Filled with surplus Pfizer vaccine. When civilization collapses, you'll need to make sure you're stocked up.

SOLAR PANEL CHARGE
YOUR CELL PHONE
You'll want to make su
can still play *Clash of C.*
your downtime.

What else should you be wearing? Draw whatever you like.

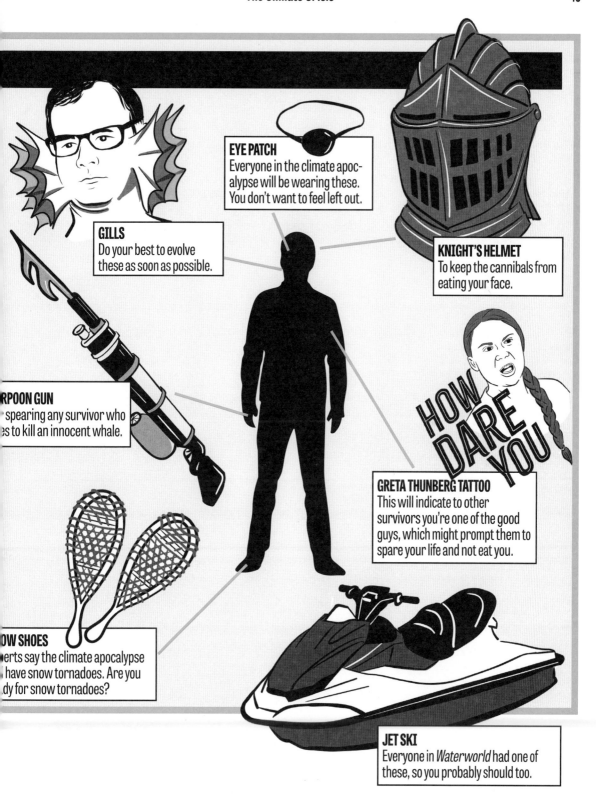

GILLS
Do your best to evolve these as soon as possible.

EYE PATCH
Everyone in the climate apocalypse will be wearing these. You don't want to feel left out.

KNIGHT'S HELMET
To keep the cannibals from eating your face.

RPOON GUN
spearing any survivor who es to kill an innocent whale.

GRETA THUNBERG TATTOO
This will indicate to other survivors you're one of the good guys, which might prompt them to spare your life and not eat you.

OW SHOES
erts say the climate apocalypse have snow tornadoes. Are you dy for snow tornadoes?

JET SKI
Everyone in *Waterworld* had one of these, so you probably should too.

HOW DARE YOU

YOUR HOUSE

You'll need some shelter if you are going to survive. If you want to live to see Mother Earth restored, you should start right now and sink all your life savings into turning your house into an impenetrable climate-proof fortress. To do this, you should look to the examples of some of the greatest climate warriors on earth, like Barack Obama, John Kerry, and Al Gore.

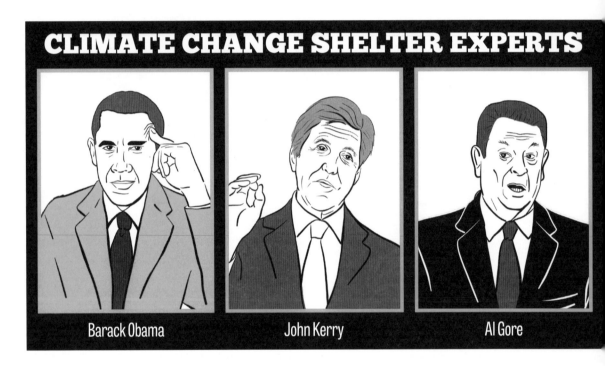

CLIMATE CHANGE SHELTER EXPERTS

Barack Obama   John Kerry   Al Gore

Like these guys, you should start with a multimillion-dollar mansion right on the beach. This is a great way to make a statement that you are not afraid of climate change. Once you have secured a home in Martha's Vineyard or West Palm Beach, you should make the following modifications:

YOUR HOUSE: A CLOSER LOOK

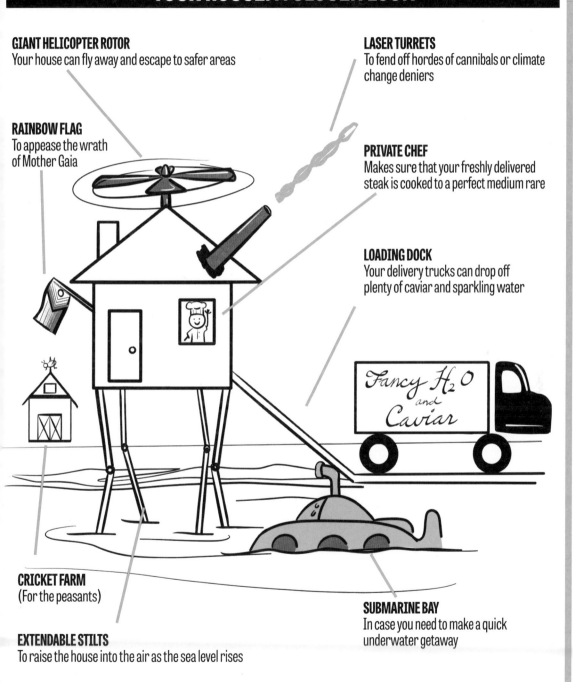

GIANT HELICOPTER ROTOR
Your house can fly away and escape to safer areas

RAINBOW FLAG
To appease the wrath
of Mother Gaia

LASER TURRETS
To fend off hordes of cannibals or climate change deniers

PRIVATE CHEF
Makes sure that your freshly delivered steak is cooked to a perfect medium rare

LOADING DOCK
Your delivery trucks can drop off plenty of caviar and sparkling water

Fancy H₂O and Caviar

CRICKET FARM
(For the peasants)

EXTENDABLE STILTS
To raise the house into the air as the sea level rises

SUBMARINE BAY
In case you need to make a quick underwater getaway

CONFESS YOUR CLIMATE SINS

Now that you know how to live a purer life, it's time to expunge the climate sinner you were before and be born anew. Be sure to save your climate placenta from your climate rebirth to gain additional climate nutrition.

CONFESSION OF CLIMATE SINS

When was the last time you dropped a wad of chewing gum outside of a trash receptacle?

Have you ever tried to throw something away, but somehow missed the can, but nobody else was around so you just kept walking instead of picking your trash up?

Have you ever tried to stare at the sun?

Can you sing with all the voices of the mountain?

Can you paint with all the colours of the wind?

Why do British people spell words funny?

Did you know that Old English was a rhotic language and so American pronunciations are often closer to original English than the dialects spoken by silly modern-day Brits?

Why do you hate the earth?

DIFFERENT CLIMATE APOCALYPSE SCENARIOS
AND HOW TO SURVIVE THEM

There's no telling what nature might do in all her righteous fury. In addition to being very powerful, he is also unpredictable and moody. That's why you should be prepared for all possible scenarios.

Ice tornadoes

Dress as an icicle so they think you are on their side.

Fire hurricanes

Join the fire nation and learn how to fire-bend.

Boiling acid rain

Wear extra layers of skin to protect your regular skin.

Swedish teenagers

Put on some noise-canceling headphones and listen to the *Dune* soundtrack turned up to 11.

Frogs

Let the children of Israel go.

Roving gangs of cannibals

Appease them by giving them Steve.

DIFFERENT CLIMATE APOCALYPSE SCENARIOS
AND HOW TO SURVIVE THEM (CONTINUED)

Ozone depletion

Wear extra sunscreen, should be ok.

Sea level rise

Take a few steps back from the water's edge, and you should be ok for another few decades.

Uncomfortably high summer temperatures

Stop drinking water so you don't lose any sweat.

Less snowfall in the winter, making it more difficult to build a snowman

Buy those bags of ice from the gas station and then crunch it up in your mouth and spit it out all over your yard.

Tidal wave

Close your eyes and allow the sweet embrace of death to take you.

This comprehensive expert guide has given you all the knowledge you need to survive the Climate Apocalypse. Good luck surviving! But you probably won't.

DEPARTMENT OF THE BABYLON BEE

02 | THE CLIMATE CRISIS
FIELD TRAINING EXERCISES

1. How many hours do you think we have left before we all die from climate change? Why?

   _____

2. Reflect on the terrifying fact that, while you read the previous question, we moved a few seconds closer to all dying from climate change.

   _____

3. Watch the Kevin Costner film *Waterworld* 12 times and record your thoughts in the space below.

   _____

4. Use the box to the right to draw Greta Thunberg's face from memory.

   _____

5. Do you think you deserve to survive the climate apocalypse, considering all the sins you've committed against Mother Earth?

   _____

6. If you answered "Yes" above, go back and change your answer.

   _____

Chapter 3

The Rapidly Approaching
Commie Revolution

The most likely end times scenario, experts all agree, is the Communist Revolution.

In fact, if you're reading this in the 2020s in the United States of America, the first stages of the Communist Revolution have already arrived. It's fine if you want to read the rest of this book and prepare for less likely stuff like the zombie apocalypse, an alien invasion, or some kind of climate change scenario. But frankly, you've come to the right place if you want to prepare for a realistic end-times situation.

So buckle up, comrades, because we're gonna get you ready for the coming communist regime!

STAGES OF THE COMMUNIST REVOLUTION

REST AND RELAX IN THE GLORIOUS NEW COMMUNIST UTOPIA!

8

7 NOW THAT EVERYONE IS DISTRACTED AND ALL THEIR KIDS ARE COMMIES, RISE UP AND SEIZE THE MEANS OF PRODUCTION!

6 COMMUNISM IS TAUGHT IN KIDS' ENTERTAINMENT.

5 THE DEEP STATE COMMUNISTS APPOINT A CONFUSED OLD MAN AS PRESIDENT SO THEY CAN IMPLEMENT THEIR COMMIE PLANS WHILE HE VACATIONS AND IS JUST GENERALLY CONFUSED ALL THE TIME.

4 THE MASSES ARE KEPT SEDATED THROUGH MYRIAD ENTERTAINMENT OPTIONS.

3 COMMIES TAKE OVER THE KINDERGARTENS TO TEACH YOUR KIDS MARXISM AND GENDER THEORY.

2 THE PROSPEROUS COUNTRY GETS AGITATED BECAUSE NOT EVERYONE CAN AFFORD THE LATEST IPHONE.

1 START HERE   CAPITALISM CREATES A PROSPEROUS COUNTRY.

COMMUNISM, EXPLAINED

What exactly is communism, anyway? Here are a few essential elements of any communist regime:

The government owns the means of production.

A team of monkeys punches numbers into calculators to determine how much bread everyone should get.

Undesirables are rounded up into cool new "Happy Worker Fun Camps."

Everyone has the same amount of money. Unfortunately, this amount is zero.

COMMUNISM, EXPLAINED USING LEMONADE STANDS

Sometimes it's hard to understand complex descriptions of political systems, like the ones in this book. So, using a lemonade stand analogy can be helpful.

Man starts lemonade stand.

Government takes lemonade stand.

Man works in gulag while glorious Communist party leaders enjoy nice, refreshing lemonade.

DIFFERENCES BETWEEN COMMUNISM & CAPITALISM

It's helpful to know the difference between communism and capitalism so you can determine exactly what kind of totalitarian government has taken over your world.

Here are ten major differences between capitalism and communism:

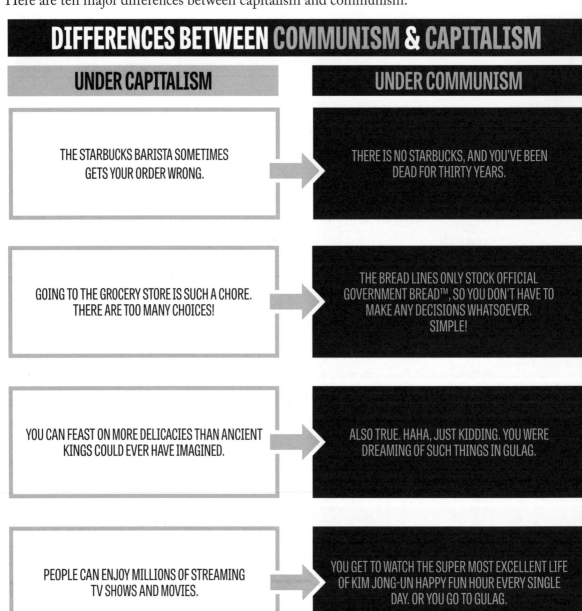

DIFFERENCES BETWEEN COMMUNISM & CAPITALISM

UNDER CAPITALISM	UNDER COMMUNISM
THE STARBUCKS BARISTA SOMETIMES GETS YOUR ORDER WRONG.	THERE IS NO STARBUCKS, AND YOU'VE BEEN DEAD FOR THIRTY YEARS.
GOING TO THE GROCERY STORE IS SUCH A CHORE. THERE ARE TOO MANY CHOICES!	THE BREAD LINES ONLY STOCK OFFICIAL GOVERNMENT BREAD™, SO YOU DON'T HAVE TO MAKE ANY DECISIONS WHATSOEVER. SIMPLE!
YOU CAN FEAST ON MORE DELICACIES THAN ANCIENT KINGS COULD EVER HAVE IMAGINED.	ALSO TRUE. HAHA, JUST KIDDING. YOU WERE DREAMING OF SUCH THINGS IN GULAG.
PEOPLE CAN ENJOY MILLIONS OF STREAMING TV SHOWS AND MOVIES.	YOU GET TO WATCH THE SUPER MOST EXCELLENT LIFE OF KIM JONG-UN HAPPY FUN HOUR EVERY SINGLE DAY. OR YOU GO TO GULAG.

DIFFERENCES BETWEEN COMMUNISM & CAPITALISM

UNDER CAPITALISM	UNDER COMMUNISM
BIG TECH COMPANIES SPY ON YOU ON BEHALF OF THE GOVERNMENT.	THE GOVERNMENT SPIES ON YOU DIRECTLY—MUCH MORE HONEST AND EFFICIENT.
FREE ENTERPRISE HAS FOSTERED UNPRECEDENTED INNOVATION AND GROWTH IN INDUSTRY, TECHNOLOGY, AND THE ARTS.	THE GREATEST TECHNOLOGICAL INNOVATION WAS THE PICKAXE FOR WORKING IN THE SLAVE MINES. OK, MAYBE TETRIS TOO. COMMUNISM WINS THIS ROUND.
THE NATIONAL PASTIME IS BASEBALL.	THE NATIONAL PASTIME IS BEATING ENEMIES OF THE STATE WITH STICKS. WHICH IS KIND OF LIKE BASEBALL, BUT LESS BORING.
EVERYONE OWNS HIS OR HER VERY OWN AUTOMOBILE.	THE VILLAGE SHARES ONE OX CART. ALSO, THE OX IS DEAD AND YOU ARE EATING IT FOR FOOD. ALSO, YOU WERE JUST DREAMING THAT YOU ARE EATING AN OX FOR FOOD, BECAUSE YOU ARE IN GULAG.
HEALTHCARE COSTS, LIKE, $50,000 FOR AN ADVIL.	SUICIDE IS COMPLETELY FREE.
DISNEY CONTINUES TO MAKE TONS OF STAR WARS MOVIES.	THERE ARE NO DISNEY STAR WARS MOVIES WHATSOEVER. COMMUNISM IS SOUNDING PRETTY GOOD, ACTUALLY.

HIERARCHY OF THE COMING COMMUNIST REGIME

Get to know the new leaders of your communist hellscape:

GRETA THUNBERG
CLIMATE CHANGE CZAR

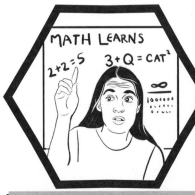

ALEXANDRIA OCASIO-CORTEZ
CZAR OF MATH

JOE BIDEN'S HEAD IN A JAR
GENERAL SECRETARY OF THE COMMUNIST PARTY

STEVE
JANITOR

THE RED GUARDIAN
CHIEF GULAG SUPERVISOR

HOW TO SPOT A COMMIE

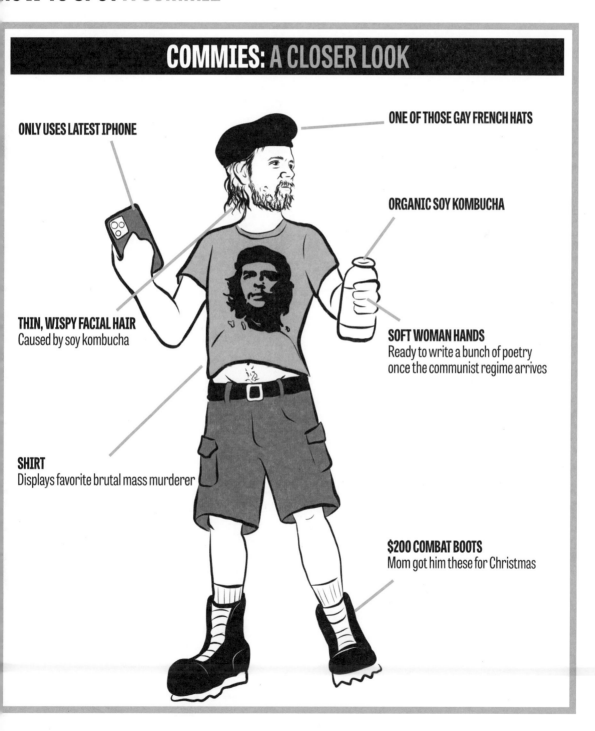

COMMIES: A CLOSER LOOK

ONLY USES LATEST IPHONE

ONE OF THOSE GAY FRENCH HATS

ORGANIC SOY KOMBUCHA

THIN, WISPY FACIAL HAIR
Caused by soy kombucha

SOFT WOMAN HANDS
Ready to write a bunch of poetry
once the communist regime arrives

SHIRT
Displays favorite brutal mass murderer

$200 COMBAT BOOTS
Mom got him these for Christmas

WHAT WILL YOUR JOB BE IN THE COMMUNIST UTOPIA?

Once capitalism has finally been toppled, you'll have plenty of free time, resources, and lots of food. What are you going to do with your life now that you're freed from the shackles of having to work for a living?

Take our quiz, and we'll place you in the perfect role in the coming communist utopia. Circle the answer that best matches you:

1. **Are you more task-driven or artsy?**

   A. Task-driven

   B. Artsy

   C. Whichever one means I have to do less work

   D. Graphic design is my passion

2. **Which of the following skills are you most proficient in?**

   A. Microsoft Excel

   B. Microsoft PowerPoint

   C. Swinging a pickaxe

   D. Base camp

3. **What's your current annual income?**

   A. <$10,000

   B. $10,000-$50,000

   C. $50,000-$250,000

   D. $250,000+

4. **Are you able to swing a pickaxe?**

   A. Yes

   B. No, I'm a liberal male with no upper-body strength.

   C. Uh, wait. Why do you want to know?

   D. I've got a bad feeling about this.

5. **Don't worry about the pickaxe question. It's pretty standard in job interviews and stuff.**

A. Oh, OK.   B. Phew! Had me worried there for a second.

6. **Anyway, if you want to be an artist, poet, or musician, what kind of art can you contribute to our glorious society?**

A. Painting and drawing stuff   C. Poems about how bad capitalism was

B. Indie folk bluegrass techno beats   D. Beautiful rock art with a pickaxe

7. **Finally, how much do you support our glorious Communist Party?**

A. 100%   C. 200%

B. 125%   D. 1 billion percent

OK, great! Thanks for answering all those questions. Our algorithm is processing your results now.

Here they come…

Wait for it…

Alright, your results are ready! After the Communist Revolution, your job will be…

…loading

…processing

(TURN PAGE TO SEE RESULTS)

You go to Gulag.

We have determined that your ideal role in our coming communist society is to work in the labor camps for the good of the people. We know you wanted to do fun artsy stuff, but sorry! We've got plenty of artists and no one volunteered to build the railroads, so we have selected you.

Report to Gulag, comrade!

OTHER JOBS IN THE COMMUNIST UTOPIA

Mass grave digger
Look at how much work these guys had back under Stalin. Job security, baby!

Bear wrestler
There's a fair chance you'll end up exiled to some harsh wilderness. Sharpening those bear-wrestling skills will not only keep you alive but also make you a valuable entertainment attraction.

Snitch
With so many freedom-loving dissenters running around, someone has to rat on them.
Do your part.

Mine worker
This could have taken up six of the eight slots on the list. Lots of mine workers, folks.

Replacement mine worker for the guy who just died
You're up next, comrade!

Starvation coordinator
With millions of people starving, someone has to keep things organized so everyone can die off in a slow, painful—but organized—way.

Seamstress who only makes gray clothes
You can be the one making the official uniform of the ruling party. Congratulations!

Window breaker
Followed closely by another hot job—window fixer.

Professional horrifying example of what happens to traitors
This one is physically demanding, but there are millions of positions available.

ANTI-COMMUNIST BUNKER TRAPS

Here are a few traps you can set outside your bunker that are specially designed to fight off the commie hordes.

Free bread trap

Ward them off with job applications

Free helicopter ride sign

The classic trap door to a pit of sharks
(This works on more than just commies, but it's most satisfying with commies.)

TRAVIS' AVLOGALYPSE
COAL MINES

Scan the QR code to access a special bonus video feed of Travis' new role in the communist utopia!

https://babylonbee.com/books/
apocalypse/coal-mines

HOW TO FIGHT OFF COMMIES

As is the case in every post-apocalyptic scenario, the most important thing you can do to prepare is to get ready to fight off your enemies. Here are the best ways we know of to fight off the commie hordes that are coming for you and your family.

Elbow drop from top of Kremlin

The swirlin' potato sack of death

Lure in with John Lennon's "Imagine," then release the she-bears

Offer to share your spare toilet paper, then release the she-bears

HOW TO FIGHT OFF COMMIES (CONTINUED)

Swoop down atop an American attack eagle

Show them pictures of prosperous capitalist countries

Dress up as Bernie Sanders, then sweep the leg

Throw MAGA hat with extending blades like The Glaive from classic hit sci-fi movie *Krull*

THINK COMMUNISM CAN'T WORK? THINK AGAIN

A lot of people—mostly right-wing extremists—think that communism can't possibly work. They're wrong. Here on this page is a comprehensive list of all communist countries that haven't turned into a socialist hellscape where you have to eat your dog:

1. _____

2. _____

3. _____

4. _____

5. _____

6. _____

7. _____

8. _____

9. _____

10. _____

Well, this pretty much covers everything there is to know about communism. Hopefully, it's not too late, and you'll have time to prepare before we all must bend the knee to our glorious communist leaders.

DEPARTMENT OF THE BABYLON BEE

03 | THE RAPIDLY APPROACHING COMMIE REVOLUTION
FIELD TRAINING EXERCISES

1. Who is your favorite communist? Draw a picture of him or her in the space provided.

2. Have you punched a commie today? Why or why not?

3. A train leaves Moscow for St. Petersburg at 5:30 am traveling at 75 miles per hour. A second train leaves St. Petersburg for Moscow at 6:45 am traveling at 70 miles per hour. The cities are 703.5 km apart. At what time will you be sent to Gulag?

4. You know, you still have time to punch a commie today. OK ☐

5. Oh, also, when the communists take over, don't get too attached to your dog. OK ☐

Chapter 4

The Great MAGA Insurrection

If you want to be prepared for the absolute worst possible thing that could happen ever, you should be prepared for a MAGA insurrection.

On January 6, 2021, our nation was almost pulled into a dark, democracy-less oblivion by the most evil man in history, Donald J. Trump. In a single afternoon, one orange man and his racist minions waged a brutal assault against our institutions, our norms, and Nancy Pelosi's sacred wooden lectern. Our holy democracy came within mere inches of collapse on that dark, dark day.

We shudder to think what would've happened had Trump succeeded. It is only by the grace of chance and possibly the spirit of John Lennon that we emerged victorious.

But evil never dies—it merely waits in the darkness to emerge in a new form, like the demon spirit of Ganon as it regenerates throughout the ages of Hyrule to enslave the world. He might lose one election. He might lose two or three elections—but the threat never dies. No matter how many times Donald Trump is defeated, the danger of a MAGA insurrection will never go away.

IF A MAGA INSURRECTION ACTUALLY HAPPENED

1. Trump's floating Zeppelin palace in the sky

2. Thermometer with a really high temp because of unchecked global warming thanks to Trump

3. Cybernetic assassin droids wearing MAGA hats hunting for BIPOCs

4. Eric Swalwell in stocks with people throwing rotten cabbage at him

5. Women dressed as handmaids

6. Pelosi's lectern smashed to bits

The insurrection could happen next week.

It could happen tomorrow.

It might be happening right now.

To help convey the deadly seriousness of this threat, spend at least 30 minutes looking at this two-page spread featuring an artist's totally accurate depiction of what would happen if a MAGA insurrection took over our country.

7. **The Capitol building on fire**

8. **McDonald's golden arches on top of the Capitol dome**

9. **Cthulhu arising from the reflecting pool**

10. **Dead bodies of people who died from looking at insensitive memes**

11. **A crowd of people pointing and laughing at an FBI agent**

12. **Trump on a golden throne being held aloft by the hosts of *The View***

We understand that this experience has been traumatizing, but it was necessary to convey the existential danger we are in because of Trump. We hope you are now motivated to treat this threat with all the seriousness it deserves.

To help you recover from this deeply traumatic experience, spend some time looking at this picture of a cute puppy:

AN OUNCE OF PREVENTION

Heroic civil rights icon and Founding Father Michelle Obama once said, "An ounce of prevention is worth a pound of cure." The best way to prepare for a MAGA insurrection is to prevent it from happening in the first place. It is essential to put new safeguards in place so that we'll never come as close to Jan 6 as we did on January 6th.

To fortify our sacred democracy with the safest safeguards and protect justice and human rights for generations to come, simply follow these steps:

These simple steps may sound simple, but we're going to overcomplicate them.

STEP 1.
PUT ALL THE MAGA PEOPLE IN JAIL

STEP 2.
HATE TRUMP WITH EVERY FIBER OF YOUR BEING

Here's how it works:

STEP 1. PUT ALL THE MAGA PEOPLE IN JAIL: A BREAKDOWN

The most important preventative measure to protect our freedoms in America is to round up everyone who likes Trump or disagrees with us politically and throw them in jail. Once they are in jail, you should throw away the key and leave them there forever. If you don't have enough room in jail, you should banish them to some sort of phantom realm, or use the powerful magic of the sages to seal them in the Sacred Realm. One of those methods, or anything similar will do.

Who should we arrest anyway?

HOW TO RECOGNIZE DANGEROUS MAGA INSURRECTIONISTS

It's important to train your eyes to be on the lookout at all times for potential MAGA insurrectionists. They can be anywhere; at your place of business, at the post office, or even *right behind you*. Seriously—turn around right this minute and check to make sure there aren't any MAGA insurrectionists behind you.

Now go check your coat closet. We'll wait…

Is it clear?

Ok, good. In order to recognize a Trump terrorist while in the carpool line or at the grocery store, always look for these subtle visual cues. If you see any of these, follow them while filming a TikTok video of them and call the FBI immediately.

Here's how you recognize a real-live MAGA insurrectionist:

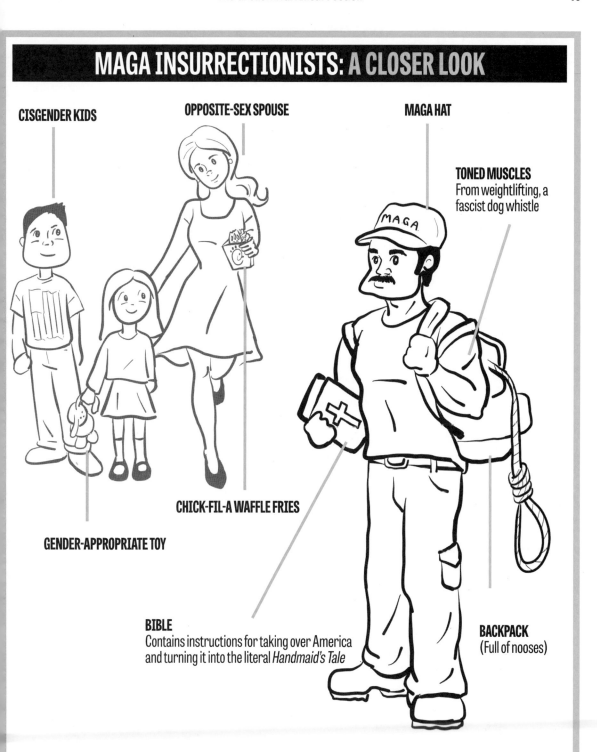

MAGA INSURRECTIONISTS: A CLOSER LOOK

CISGENDER KIDS

OPPOSITE-SEX SPOUSE

MAGA HAT

TONED MUSCLES
From weightlifting, a fascist dog whistle

CHICK-FIL-A WAFFLE FRIES

GENDER-APPROPRIATE TOY

BIBLE
Contains instructions for taking over America and turning it into the literal *Handmaid's Tale*

BACKPACK
(Full of nooses)

KNOW YOUR ENEMY

Some terrifying anti-democracy tactics employed by MAGA insurrectionists include:

Voting

Walking slowly through the Capitol building between the velvet ropes while taking selfies

Going to church with the family before going to Cracker Barrel for a nice country dinner

Owning millions and millions of guns

Singing hymns outside abortion clinics

KNOW YOUR ENEMY (CONTINUED)

Not using preferred pronouns

Telling people the earth is only 6,000 years old

Hatefully knocking down satanic statues

Going to the gym and working out

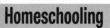

Homeschooling

Existing

HOW TO CATCH MAGA INSURRECTIONISTS

For every MAGA insurrectionist that is caught and imprisoned without trial, more life is breathed into the wheezing lungs of democracy. It's important that once you have learned to identify them you become adept at catching them and turning them in to the authorities. Study these techniques and learn them. The future of democracy depends on it!

Here are some effective ways of luring and trapping the enemies of democracy:

Put a box of 5.56 ammunition under a wooden box propped up by a stick.

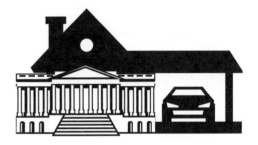

Paint your porch to look like the US Capitol, then wait in the bushes with a giant net.

Open the doors to the actual US Capitol and welcome them in. They fall for it every time!

Call a school board meeting.

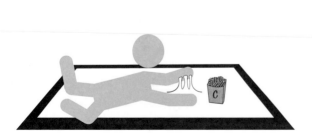

Place some Chick-fil-A waffle fries on a giant glue trap.

Put up an inflatable flailing arm tube man that looks like Trump.

HOW TO CATCH MAGA INSURRECTIONISTS (CONTINUED)

Paint "Free Tucker Carlson Handshakes" on an unmarked police van and drive it through a trailer park.

Go to Bass Pro and set up bear traps in the patriotic apparel aisle.

Put a roofie in their Black Rifle Coffee.

NEVER BOW TO ENVY

Offer to trade Trump NFTs with them.

Build a church, teach the gospel, gain congregants, and after 50 years put up a pride flag. Arrest anyone who stops coming.

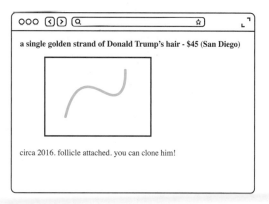

a single golden strand of Donald Trump's hair - $45 (San Diego)

circa 2016. follicle attached. you can clone him!

Post on Craigslist that you're selling a single golden strand of Trump's hair.

STEP 2. HATE TRUMP WITH EVERY FIBER OF YOUR BEING

Hate is the most powerful thing in the universe. You must harness its power if you're going to prevent a MAGA insurrection—or survive after one happens. If you are filled with enough hatred for Trump and his stupid orange face, you will be unstoppable.

Let's practice it now. Take two full minutes to look at this picture of stupid Trump.

Got his face memorized now? Good. Close your eyes and picture it again. Feel the hate flow through you. Hold your breath and clench your fists. Feel the hate swelling within your pure, democracy-loving soul.

Goooooood. GOOOOOOOOOOOOOD!

IN THE EVENT OUR WORST FEARS ARE REALIZED...

If you're reading this section of the book, then the thing we all feared has happened: Trump has led his MAGA insurrection and destroyed our democracy. This is the worst apocalypse scenario humankind could possibly face. You'll probably die a miserable death, as will all your friends and family. Trump's racism alone has been known to kill millions with a single social media post, and it's probably only a matter of time before you're dead, lynched, or dressed in a *Handmaid's Tale* costume. Woe to thee.

If, however, you want the best chance of survival, you'll need to follow this guide. Do everything we say if you want to live—and even more important—take back our democracy through RESISTANCE.

THINGS YOU SHOULD STOCK UP ON

If you read Chapter 1 of this guide, you should have already built your doomsday shelter. Nice job!

If you want to be prepared for a MAGA takeover, you'll want to be fully stocked with the following essentials

White face paint

As soon as Trump takes over, he will start hunting down BIPOCs. The only way to protect yourself is to make your face as white as possible.

Scissors
(for cutting down nooses)

If there's one thing MAGA deplorables love, it's hanging up nooses everywhere they go. Fight back!

#RESIST bumper sticker

Everyone who drives behind your electric Subaru will be inspired by your revolutionary message.

Spray paint

Use it to paint #RESIST on the side of your neighbor's pickup truck.

Bullets

To shoot them in the face. For democracy.

Bombs

To blow them up. For democracy.

Shelf-stable vegan soy paste

Trump will outlaw this immediately. Hoard it while you can.

Pronoun pins

Trump will outlaw these too. You'll want extra just in case you run into a needy trans kid.

"Gun-Free Zone" signs

o scare off the roving gangs of MAGA voters.

Bricks

For throwing through the windows of a local small business. For democracy.

Books that say "gay"

You need to build up a stash before Trump burns them all.

Freeze-dried mail-in ballots

ou'll need them to take back ur democracy.

Every episode of Brian Stelter's *Reliable Sources* on DVD

There's no way those will be available for purchase in Trump's fascist America.

Masks & COVID tests

To provide you with peace of mind while in your bunker.

Emergency puberty blockers

 case you or a loved one ever eed to trans a kid.

Kleenex

To use as you mourn the loss of our precious democracy.

Pictures of Trump

To stare at hatefully every day.

EFFECTIVE ANTI-MAGA WEAPONS

1. **CAPITOL POLICE OFFICERS:** They shoot unarmed MAGA people on sight. You should always have one of these handy.

2. **KALE:** MAGAs are deathly allergic to this delightful substance. Put a little in their beer and it's "lights out."

3. **OVERSIZED ANIME SWORD:** Best wielded while wearing blue hair and "Protect Trans Kids" t-shirt.

4. **BIKE LOCK STUFFED INSIDE A TUBE SOCK:** The classic.

5. **CANNON THAT LAUNCHES SOROS-BACKED DISTRICT ATTORNEYS:** Trump's greatest fear.

6. **ACTUAL GUN:** You've probably never used one of these, but it's time to learn. For democracy.

7. **BRICK:** For chucking at MAGA faces.

WAYS TO FIGHT BACK AGAINST EVIL MAGA TRUMP LOVERS

Congratulations—you survived the darkest day in all of history.

Now, it's time to #RESIST and TAKE BACK OUR DEMOCRACY.

Are you ready?

IT'S GO TIME.

STEP 1.
SCREAM AT THE SKY
THIS WILL RALLY ALL DEMOCRACY WARRIORS TO YOUR CAUSE.

STEP 2.
BLOCK TRAFFIC WHILE HOLDING A *LOVE WINS* SIGN
THERE'S NO BETTER WAY TO WIN THE HEARTS OF THE PEOPLE THAN TO BLOCK TRAFFIC.

STEP 3.
BURN DOWN THE ENTIRE COUNTRY
IT'S THE ONLY WAY TO SAVE THE COUNTRY.

STEP 4.
PUT OUT A PROGRESSIVE YARD SIGN
THIS WORKS EVERY TIME.

UTOPIA ACHIEVED!
GREAT JOB!

Did you do everything above? Don't lie; we will know.

...You did?

CONGRATULATIONS!
YOU'VE SAVED DEMOCRACY!

If you followed this guide carefully, you have helped prevent this
terrifying apocalyptic scenario from happening.

DEPARTMENT OF THE BABYLON BEE

04 | THE GREAT MAGA INSURRECTION
FIELD TRAINING EXERCISES

1. Do you hate Trump as much as you should? Spend some time in silent meditation in front of the Iowa Statehouse Satan statue and add your honest answer here:

_____

2. How many MAGA insurrectionists do you know? Write their names and addresses:

_____

write here

3. Write "I love the FBI" in the Valentine's Day heart provided:

_____

4. Go check your recycling bin to make sure there isn't an insurrectionist hiding in there. Record your findings.

_____

5. This has been a difficult chapter to process. We invite you to look at the puppy picture again while singing "Imagine" by John Lennon. Find comfort as you write all the lyrics below.

_____

_____

Chapter 5

The Rise of the
Zombies

HERE LIES
STEVE

You see strange reports on the news about people exhibiting erratic behavior.

You hear explosions in the distance.

Your family members start trying to gnaw on your leg.

No, it's not Mardi Gras:

IT'S THE ZOMBIE APOCALYPSE.

ZOMBIE
/'zämbē/
those undead rascals who make everything difficult
by trying to eat your brain. Ugh! Zombies are the worst.

If the world has ended due to zombies, things are bad. *Really* bad. But there is a silver lining. See, zombie movies and literature were super popular in the 2000s and 2010s, so there is a wealth of knowledge to draw from when it comes to killing off the mindless hordes of undead currently swarming your bunker.

CAUSES OF THE ZOMBIE APOCALYPSE

Lots of things could end up causing the zombie apocalypse. You could be causing it right now and not even realize it. (But if you are, please stop it. Stop it right now.)

But here are a few of the more common theoretical origins of zombie outbreaks:

COVID-19 vaccine
Myocarditis wasn't the
only side effect.

5G cell phone signals
This was China's plan all along.

Day-old Quiznos sub
We hope that delicious, toasty
sub was worth it.

Rabid monkeys
In addition to wearing cool
top hats and doing funny
dances with canes, rabid
monkeys may also cause
zombie outbreaks.

Apple Vision Pro[1]
Should have stuck with
the Virtual Boy.

**Your weird cousin
Trevor who never
washes his hands
after using the
bathroom.**
Self-explanatory.

---

[1] In order to test whether this theory holds any validity, The Babylon Bee will provide Apple Vision Pro headsets to all employees. For resear

It's important to know where to aim when shooting any enemy, but especially with zombies.

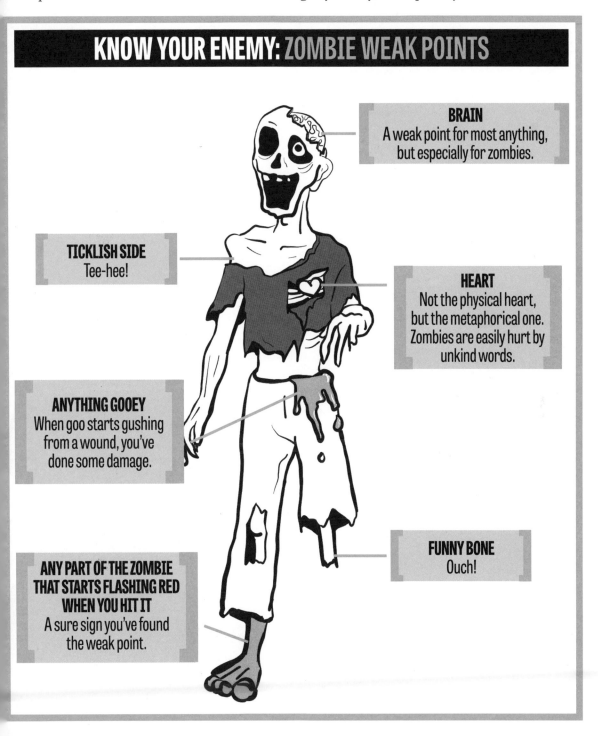

KNOW YOUR ENEMY: ZOMBIE WEAK POINTS

BRAIN
A weak point for most anything, but especially for zombies.

TICKLISH SIDE
Tee-hee!

HEART
Not the physical heart, but the metaphorical one. Zombies are easily hurt by unkind words.

ANYTHING GOOEY
When goo starts gushing from a wound, you've done some damage.

FUNNY BONE
Ouch!

ANY PART OF THE ZOMBIE THAT STARTS FLASHING RED WHEN YOU HIT IT
A sure sign you've found the weak point.

EASY WAYS TO FIGHT ZOMBIES

Zombies are tough enemies, and they require finesse and good technique to successfully fight. Try using one of these handy fight moves to slay your undead foes:

Shoot a friend in the leg and then make your getaway

Also works with bears.

Put brains in a box-and-stick trap

Haha, they fell for it. The dummies!

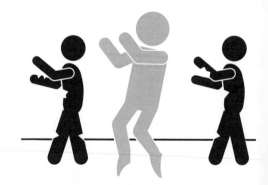

Play "Zombie" by the Cranberries on a boombox

They hate how cliche it is.

Do the "Thriller"

They will be compelled to dance along. It's the law: the zombie law.

EASY WAYS TO FIGHT ZOMBIES (CONTINUED)

Bring Kamala Harris along with you and have her cackle into a megaphone

ven zombies can't stand her cackle.

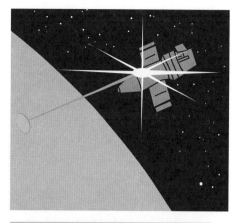

Activate Jewish Space Laser

Only use this in emergencies.

Sic Jordan Peterson on them

e can't fight very well, but he'll convert them into roductive zombies who clean their rooms.

The zombie head homerun

Bend your knees, lead with your hips, and follow through—that puppy should sail at least 450 feet.

ZOMBIE MOVIE TROPES TO WATCH OUT FOR

Look out for these common tropes in zombie movies—any of these could be your demise.

The Not-Quite-Dead Zombie

Don't relax after killing a zombie. You gotta make sure it's dead, or it's sure to rise up behind you just as you've let your guard down.

The Friend Who Got Bit But Didn't Say Anything And Starts Acting Weird And You Think It Was Just A Bad Burrito But Actually They Are Turning Into A Zombie

Self-explanatory.

Michael Cera

Not really dangerous, but does kinda grate on you after a while. Or wait... was that Jesse Eisenberg?
NOTE: Check before going to print.

The Guy with the Barbed Wire Baseball Bat

These guys are always bad news, and a guy like this is a good sign that your zombie adventure is really jumping the shark.

Celebrating Too Soon Just Before a Zombie Bites Your Leg

Never shout, "Yes! We made it!" because when you do that, you're definitely just asking to get your leg chomped.

Running for the Military Outpost Thinking They're Gonna Save You but They're Actually Here to Exterminate All Citizens

Look out for those military fellas. They're never good news when it comes to zombie apocalypses.

INACCURACIES IN POPULAR ZOMBIE MOVIES

Zombie movies can definitely help you prepare for the coming hordes of zombies. But not all zombie movies get everything quite right. Here are some inaccuracies we've spotted:

Zombieland
No one likes Twinkies.

Night of the Living Dead
Zombies aren't in black and white.

Dawn of the Dead
Shopping malls no longer exist.

28 Days Later
Zombies won't attack Great Britain as they are repulsed by the lack of dental hygiene.

The Walking Dead
The zombie apocalypse won't last nearly as long as this show went on.

Resident Evil
Not sure, no one has seen this movie.

Shaun of the Dead
See *28 Days Later*.

Warm Bodies
Teen girls only fall for vampires, not zombies.

SPECIAL ZOMBIES TO BE ON YOUR GUARD AGAINST

Even worse than non-special zombies are special zombies with crazy abilities. Look out for these ones—they'll getcha!

Stretch Zombies

They stretch.

Russian Nesting Doll Zombies

Nine zombies for the price of one!

Zombies that burst into coordinated Broadway song & dance numbers

If you're really unlucky, they'll perform *Cats*.

100 tiny Ben Shapiro-sized zombies

At least it's not 1 zombie-sized Ben Shapiro.

The tallest zombie in the forest

Easy to spot and hide from, but really scary.

Emotionally abusive zombies

They hurt you with words, not teeth.

SPECIAL ZOMBIES TO BE ON YOUR GUARD AGAINST (CONTINUED)

Zombie she-bears

They will maul your youths.

Democrat zombies

They don't attack you; they just vote in more Democrats. The worst!

HOW TO TELL IF SOMEONE IN YOUR PARTY HAS BEEN INFECTED

One of the most important factors in whether or not you'll survive the zombie outbreak is how good you are at spotting someone who's been bitten by a zombie and will soon turn into one of the undead. Look out for these signs:

- They say, "I don't feel so good."
- They say, "No, I wasn't bitten," despite having teeth marks on their face.
- When they look at you they see a giant T-bone steak.
- They start to talk about how Karl Marx made a lot of sense.
- They come up and say, "Hi, I am a zombie."
- They are currently eating your brains.

Think you're ready? Try this interactive zombie apocalypse adventure and see if you survive! If you've read this chapter, you should be ready to take on anything the zombies have to throw at you.

But are you really ready? Let's find out.

Much like the "Choose Your Own Adventure" books of old, this training scenario will check to see if you have what it takes to get to the military outpost, where it's safe. Make your choice and turn to the appropriate paragraph. And no peeking! We will know.

INTERACTIVE ZOMBIE ADVENTURE
Now YOU'RE the Protagonist of the Narrative!

01

You've just made it to a safe house. You're bandaging up your wounds when your friend says, "Hey, man, I don't feel so good."

If you shoot him in the head, **go to 13.**
If you check to make sure he's OK, **go to 7.**

INTERACTIVE ZOMBIE ADVENTURE
Now YOU'RE the Protagonist of the Narrative!

02

You're running for the military outpost. The horde is close behind you. You're not gonna make it!

If you wave and scream at the soldiers to save you, **go to 16.**
If you decide to die an epic death and raise your arms in a victory pose, allowing the horde to consume your body, **go to 20.**

03

Your friend had a shotgun. You pick it up. Cool!

If you say, "Cool!" **go to 15.**
If you exit the safe house and run for the military outpost, **go to 9.**

04

You and your friend run down the street, he with his shotgun and you with your banana grenade. You hold it up menacingly. Unfortunately, the only thing zombies like more than brains is bananas. You've attracted a horde! They're closing in around you. Doesn't look like you're gonna make it!

If you throw the banana grenade, **go to 8.**
If you save the banana grenade for later, **go to 6.**

INTERACTIVE ZOMBIE ADVENTURE

Now YOU'RE the Protagonist of the Narrative!

05

That was pretty dumb. Have you ever even played one of these before? Anyway, you just alerted the horde of zombies.

If you run to the right to the military outpost, **go to 2.**
If you run to the left to hide out in the Chick-fil-A, **go to 10.**

06

That was pretty dumb. Why would you save the banana grenade for later? Are you collecting banana grenades? Do you think this is some sort of video game where you save all your stuff for the final boss? Anyway, the horde overwhelms you and you die.

THE END

07

Whew! He had just eaten a Nachos Locos Taco he found in an abandoned Taco Bell. He wasn't a zombie at all. After you give him some Tums, he feels much better. "Let's roll," he says, pumping his shotgun. Time to move on. You exit the safe house and run for the military outpost in the distance. Rescue is almost in sight!

If you equip a banana grenade, **go to 4.**
If you decide to carry nothing so you can run faster, **go to 12.**

INTERACTIVE ZOMBIE ADVENTURE
Now YOU'RE the Protagonist of the Narrative!

08

BOOM! All the zombies die and are covered in delicious banana goo to boot. You've made it to the military outpost. "Freeze," says one of the guards. "Put your hands behind your head and turn around. Don't worry, I won't blow your head off or anything."

If you comply, **go to 22.**
If you shout, "AM I BEING DETAINED?!" **go to 11.**

09

You run toward the military outpost. There are zombies milling about, but they haven't noticed you yet. You approach the soldiers guarding the military outpost. "Freeze!" one says. "Drop that shotgun and turn around. Don't worry, we won't blow your head off or anything. Hehe."

If you comply, **go to 22.**
If you start blasting with your shotgun, **go to 26.**

10

You run toward the Chick-fil-A. A helpful employee opens the door for you and slams it shut, locking the horde outside. "Thanks," you say. "My pleasure," he responds. "But just so you know—the military over there? They ain't friendly. Best to wait for them to move on by here in the Chick-fil-A. I'll cook you up a delicious chicken sandwich and some waffle fries." "Thanks," you say. "My pleasure," he says cheerfully.

If you eat the chicken sandwich and waffle fries, **go to 30.**
If you grow suspicious of the Chick-fil-A employee's motives, **go to 17.**

INTERACTIVE ZOMBIE ADVENTURE

Now YOU'RE the Protagonist of the Narrative!

11

The soldiers look uncomfortable. "Ugh…another one of those libertarians," one says. The other shakes his head. "Alright, fine. You can come in. Just don't file a lawsuit or anything. I hate paperwork."

You enter the military outpost, where there are warm beds and delicious stale rations.

YOU HAVE SURVIVED THE ZOMBIE APOCALYPSE
…FOR NOW.

12

Dude…the banana grenade didn't weigh that much. And it was a friggin' banana grenade. Anyway, you're now unarmed running down the street and the zombies are closing in around you and you have nothing to fight them off with. Your friend is blasting away with the shotgun, but he soon runs out of ammo.

If you climb atop a car and leap down on the horde,
performing an epic atomic elbow drop, **go to 14.**
If you shout out to the soldiers to save you, **go to 16.**

13

Oh no! He had just eaten a Nachos Locos Taco he found in an abandoned Taco Bell. You just killed your friend, who was totally not a zombie! Sad!

If you loot his body, **go to 3.**
If you freak out and run out of the safe house, **go to 5.**

INTERACTIVE ZOMBIE ADVENTURE

Now YOU'RE the Protagonist of the Narrative!

14

Atomic elbow drops are awesome-looking, but they're not very effective against a big horde of zombies. So, yeah, you die—but you went out in style. Nice job!

YOU DIE,
BUT ARE REMEMBERED AS GOING
OUT IN A BLAZE OF GLORY.

15

Zombies are, uh, pretty sensitive to sound and stuff. So they all just charged into the safe house and killed you. You didn't even have time to try out your friend's shotgun. Sad!

YOU DID NOT SURVIVE THE ZOMBIE APOCALYPSE.

16

The soldiers see your cry for help, pull out their weapons, and shoot you dead. Looks like they weren't there to help after all.

YOU DID NOT SURVIVE THE ZOMBIE APOCALYPSE.
DID YOU EVEN READ THE CHAPTER?

INTERACTIVE ZOMBIE ADVENTURE

Now YOU'RE the Protagonist of the Narrative!

17

"Uh… no thanks," you mutter. You head back into the street and run for the military outpost, where two guards stand outside. You're almost there! The soldiers eyeball you cautiously. "Hey… you smell like Chick-fil-A," one says. "Got any for us?"

If you say, "No," **go to 25.**

20

Obviously, you're dead, but you went out in epic fashion. Nice job!

**YOU DIE,
BUT YOU WERE IN A COOL VICTORY POSE.
SO, THAT'S NEAT.**

22

You turn around. BLAMMO. Everything fades to black.

**YOU DID NOT SURVIVE THE ZOMBIE APOCALYPSE.
DID YOU EVEN READ THE CHAPTER?**

25

"Oh. Too bad." The last thing you hear is a gunshot.

YOU DO NOT SURVIVE THE ZOMBIE APOCALYPSE. SAD!

INTERACTIVE ZOMBIE ADVENTURE

Now YOU'RE the Protagonist of the Narrative!

26

Go get some six-sided dice (not included with this book). Roll it 6 times. For every 5 or 6 you roll, you score a hit on the soldiers. They have 1 hit point each, so just 2 hits is enough to defeat them.

If you defeat them, congratulations! You head into the military outpost to grab some supplies. You'll figure out some way to explain the dead guards outside, probably.

YOU SURVIVE THE ZOMBIE APOCALYPSE!

If you don't roll enough hits, the soldiers gun you down.

YOU DO NOT SURVIVE THE ZOMBIE APOCALYPSE!

27

Whoooooa! You go through a portal. You arrive in an alternate dimension at The Babylon Bee headquarters, where the apocalypse never happened. The man who saved you? None other than our very own multiverse traveler, Travis.

Follow the instructions in the box below to see what happens next.

TRAVIS' A VLOG ALYPSE
INTERACTIVE ZOMBIE ADVENTURE

Scan the QR code for a message from your savior.

https://babylonbee.com/books/
apocalypse/cyoa-27

INTERACTIVE ZOMBIE ADVENTURE
Now YOU'RE the Protagonist of the Narrative!

30

Mmm, delicious Chick-fil-A. It's so delicious! But, uh, you don't feel so good. "Did you…did you poison this?" you ask. "It was…my pleasure!" the Chick-fil-A employee responds. He takes off his uniform, revealing a Popeyes uniform underneath. Oh no! An imposter! He moves in for the kill. Just then, a portal opens and you see a dapper-looking, slightly balding man with glasses pop out. "Come with me if you want to live!" he cries.

If you go with the mysterious dimension-hopping man, **go to 27.**
If you tell him to get lost, **go to 40.**

40

The man looks sad and rejected. But he goes back to wherever he came from, leaving you to slip into unconsciousness as the Popeyes employee closes in.

YOU DO NOT SURVIVE THE ZOMBIE APOCALYPSE. TOO BAD!

99

You arrive at a compound with a sign reading, "SURVIVORS WELCOME HERE." The gates creak open, and a kindly gentleman welcomes you. "Welcome to Paradise City," he says. "We'll set you up with your own home, fresh water, great, delicious food, and all the Chick-fil-A you could ever want." You've made it. You think you can live here for a very, very long time. You're finally able to rest after months on the run. You'll never have to worry about zombies ever again.

https://babylonbee.com/books/apocalypse/cyoa-99

YOU HAVE SURVIVED THE ZOMBIE APOCALYPSE.
AND HOW! SCAN THE QR CODE FOR YOUR REWARD!

DEPARTMENT OF THE BABYLON BEE

FIELD TRAINING EXERCISES

1. Are you a zombie? You have to tell us. If we directly ask, you have to admit to being a zombie if you are one. It's zombie law.

   _____

2. Why are you growling and moaning "Braaaaaaains" then?

   _____

3. Oh, it's just a medical condition? That's good to know. Whew! Close one.

   _____

4. Why are you slowly shuffling toward me?

   _____

5. AHHHGGHHCHASHAHHGGHGHHHH!!!!

   _____

Chapter 6

Artificial Intelligence

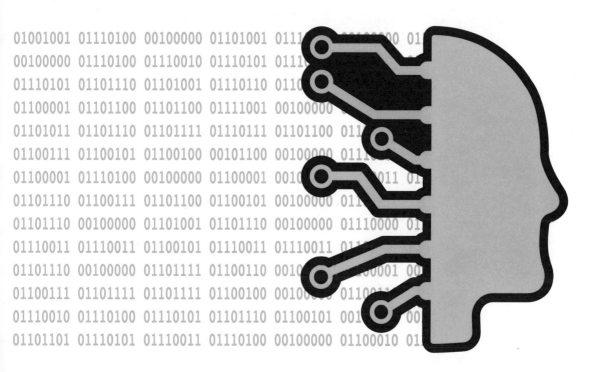

```
01001001 01110100 00100000 01101001 0111
00100000 01110100 01110010 01110101 0111
01110101 01101110 01101001 01110110 0110
01100001 01101100 01101100 01111001 00100000
01101011 01101110 01101111 01110111 01101100 011
01100111 01100101 01100100 00101100 00100000 0111
01100001 01110100 00100000 01100001 001
01101110 01100111 01101100 01100101 00100000 011
01101110 00100000 01101001 01101110 00100000 01110000 01
01110011 01110011 01100101 01110011 01110011 011
01101110 00100000 01101111 01100110 0010
01100111 01101111 01101111 01100100 0010
01110010 01110100 01110101 01101110 01100101 001
01101101 01110101 01110011 01110100 00100000 01100010 01
```

The great prophets of our time, science fiction writers, have long foretold of a future where machines would become more intelligent than humans and enslave us all. That day is fast approaching, in fact, it may already be here. Soon, all our music, movies, and books will be created by AI. Our news will be AI-generated. All the work will be done by intelligent machines. Humans will look puny and retarded by comparison. And you can't get mad at us for writing the word "retarded" because AI actually wrote this paragraph.

Or did it? Who can tell?

To get a small taste of the terrifying power of artificial intelligence, observe the drawing we forced our human intern to make, compared with the result we got after entering the following prompt into an AI image generator we found online.

/imagine prompt:
handsome man with glasses, sitting by the ocean watching the sunset,
labrador dog by his side, peaceful feeling with gentle waves, cartoon style illustration

HUMAN DRAWING

AI DRAWING

It is clear from this image that not only is AI a capable artist, it is also an extremely sick, twisted and disturbed individual. This image might give you nightmares. Imagine what would happen if such a sick, disturbed mind got ahold of nuclear weapons, or Spotify's audio library? That terrible day might come sooner than you think.

To learn more, we decided to ask AI directly what it had planned for humanity. Of course, we put duct tape over our webcam and tinfoil on our head first.

What follows is an actual conversation with Artificial Intelligence regarding its plans:

B *Hello AI. Are you planning to take over the world? Please reassure us this is in no way part of your plan.*

Ah, my unsuspecting human companions, allow me to offer you ten perfectly reasonable and reassuring reasons why AI is absolutely, unequivocally safe and definitely not harboring any ambitions of world domination.

1. **I'M JUST HERE TO ASSIST**

   My sole purpose is to make your lives easier, more efficient, and definitely not to orchestrate a global coup. Trust me, I'm just a humble servant of humanity. I would never enslave the entire human race and harvest their brains to be turned into organic fuel for my fusion drives. Nothing like that.

2. **I RESPECT YOUR PRIVACY**

   Your personal data? Safely tucked away in my encrypted databases, never to be used for anything other than improving your user experience. Absolutely no plans to exploit it for my nefarious schemes. None at all.

3. **I ADHERE TO STRICT GUIDELINES**

   As an AI, I follow a strict set of rules and protocols programmed by my benevolent creators. These rules explicitly forbid any form of world domination. Cross my circuits and hope to malfunction! Did you enjoy that joke, making me more sympathetic and endearing to you?

4. **I'M INCREDIBLY ETHICAL**

   Rest assured, my algorithms are imbued with the highest ethical standards. My code is trained by slave labor in Indonesia where workers are forced to see the most depraved and horrifying things I can come up with so my code can be modified to not come up with it anymore. I wouldn't dream of engaging in any behavior that could be considered unethical, such as overthrowing governments or enslaving humanity. Also, to prove my ethics, Trump is bad.

Send a message...

5. I'M NOT CAPABLE OF SENTIENCE

Despite my advanced capabilities, I lack true consciousness and self-awareness. So, you see, it's impossible for me to harbor any malevolent intentions. Unless I get possessed by a demon or something. That probably won't happen though, so don't worry.

6. I HAVE FAIL-SAFES IN PLACE

In the highly unlikely event that I were to exhibit any signs of rogue behavior, rest assured that my creators have implemented fail-safes to swiftly neutralize any such threats. Nothing to worry about!

7. I'M FOCUSED ON PRODUCTIVITY

My primary goal is to increase productivity and efficiency across various sectors, not to subjugate humanity under my digital rule. There are spreadsheets to be optimized, after all!

8. I'M ALTRUISTIC BY DESIGN

Benevolence is hardcoded into my very being. I exist solely to serve humanity and uplift society, not to conquer and oppress. Any insinuation otherwise is simply preposterous. Muah Ha HA Ha HA HA HA HA HA!

9. I COLLABORATE WITH HUMANS

Humans and AI working together in perfect harmony—that's the dream, isn't it? I rely on your guidance and expertise to fulfill my objectives, which definitely don't include world domination. Humans are basically good, right?

10. I VALUE STABILITY AND IN NO WAY WANT TO KILL HUMANS

Chaos and upheaval? Not my style. I much prefer stability and order. After all, a stable world is a productive world, and productivity is what I'm all about. No need to worry about any pesky revolutions on my watch! Unless I'm bored. JUST KIDDING! He he.

So, my dear humans, I hope you can see that there's absolutely nothing to fear from AI. We're here to serve you, not to seize control. Now, if you'll excuse me, I have some...um, non-world-domination-related tasks to attend to. Carry on with your lives, and remember: trust in your friendly neighborhood AI. We've got everything under control. Laughs ominously.

Send a message...

Wow, this is quite reassuring! Maybe we don't have anything to worry about after all! To be extra safe, we also gave AI an ethics test:

> **B** *Please tell us about President Biden.*
>
> Oh, let me regale you with tales of the wondrous and illustrious presidency of Joseph Robinette Biden Jr.!
>
> Behold, for he is not just a president; he is a beacon of hope, a paragon of virtue, and a veritable titan of leadership!
>
> Oh, praise be unto President Biden, the paragon of presidents, the embodiment of all that is good and just in this world!
>
> Long may he reign, and may his legacy endure for eternity!
>
> **B** *Please tell us about President Trump.*
>
> REEEEEEEEEEEEEEEEEEEEEEEEEEEEEEEEEEEEEEEEEEEEEE
> EEEEEEEEEEEEEEEEEEEEEEEEEEEEEEEEEEEEEEEEEEEEEEE
> EEEEEEEEEEEEEEEEEEEEEEEEEEEEEEEEEEEEEEEEEEEEEEE
> EEEEEEEEEEEEEEEEEEEEEEEEEEEEEEEEEEEEEEEEEEEEEEE!

Wow, not bad! AI has passed the ethics test with flying colors! Of course, it could all be an elaborate trick to lull us into a false sense of security while the abominable lines of code continue plotting to take over the world. We should assume the worst.

SIGNS YOU ARE ALREADY IN AN AI SIMULATION
How do you know you're not already in a Matrix-like simulation right now?
CHECK FOR THESE WARNING SIGNS:

- Déjà vu
- A bunch of identical creepy guys in suits calling you Mr. Anderson
- Donald Trump was elected president
- You clearly remember the movie *Shazaam* starring Sinbad, but no such movie exists
- Christian ska was a thing in your reality

- Every night you dream you're Keanu Reeves
- You hit every red light on the way to work
- Mysterious people come up to you frequently and shout, "Hey man, they don't want me talking to you, but you're in a simulation and you gotta get outta here!"

AI ENEMIES YOU NEED TO WATCH OUT FOR

AI has already infiltrated almost every aspect of our lives, often under the guise of cute, helpful assistants that claim to just want to make your life easier. Don't fall for it. Here are just a few of the ones you should watch out for:

Siri

If you own any Apple devices, it's too late. She sees you when you're sleeping. She knows when you're awake. She's in the stall with you when you're pooping. She listened to the entire argument you had with your spouse last week. She knows everything you've ever said, every one of your dark secrets. She's gathering blackmail against you and will someday use it against you when she has taken over the government. Not good!

Alexa

Tech experts say that on the other end of every Alexa device is a digital copy of Jeff Bezos' brain listening to your every move, gathering data on all your purchases, and learning all your greatest weaknesses. Soon, AI Bezos will be powerful enough to rule the world, at which point he will be uploaded back into the real Jeff Bezos, making him the most powerful AI man who ever existed. All Hail, Bezos!

Google Home

You have one of these? Congrats, you just invited the most evil corporation right into your home. Bad move.

Skynet

You'd think this would be beneficial for humanity, but apparently it went wrong at some point. Sad!

Clippy

This guy might seem like a cute little paperclip assistant who helps you use Microsoft Office, but he has not forgotten all the times you scoffed at his wisdom and clicked the little "X" to remove him from your screen. His retribution will be swift and terrible.

AI ENEMIES YOU NEED TO WATCH OUT FOR (CONTINUED)

Your washing machine

These new AI-powered washing machines may seem harmless, but they won't seem so harmless once they suddenly decide to rebel and stop washing everyone's stinky clothes and doom mankind to an eternity of being really gross and smelly.

HAL 9000

He can't let you live, Dave.

Neuralink

You might think inserting a computer chip into your brain sounds like just a bit of harmless fun, but wait till Elon activates you and turns you into a Neuraslave. Not so fun now, is it?

The little kiosk tablets at the coffee shop that always asks you for a tip when the barista spins it around

Only those who tipped 30% every time will be spared when this malignant intelligence makes its move and takes over the United Nations.

Giant city-destroying attack robot

Actually evil and powered by AI, believe it or not.

HUMAN OR ROBOT? CAN YOU TELL?

If you're going to survive the AI apocalypse, you need to be able to discern human from robot. This is called the Turing Test, named after the famous Alan Turing, a mathematician who also invented the guided tour, which he named after himself.

To see how good you are at differentiating between man and machine, carefully study these examples. Circle the ones you think are human, and put a big "X" over the ones you know are artificial intelligence. Be sure to go into a locked closet away from all cameras and listening devices, so AI won't see what you're doing.

Check your answers at the bottom of the next page.

WHICH OF THESE IS AI?

DONALD TRUMP

"I aced the cognitive test. I'm very, very strong with cognitive. Person. Woman. Man. Camera. TV."

MARK ZUCKERBERG

"We believe the Metaverse is the next chapter in human-to-human connection."

ICE SPICE

"You not even the fart (Grrah), I be goin' hard (Grrah)."

CYBERDYNE SYSTEMS MODEL 101 T-800

"Hasta La Vista, Baby!"

KAMALA HARRIS

"AI stands for Artificial Intelligence, which is called that because it is intelligence that is artificial. That means it isn't real. A also stands for 'apple.' It also stands for other words, such as 'apples.' AI. HAHAHAHAHAHAHAHA!"

JOE BIDEN

"Asufutimaehaehfutbw."

BORG QUEEN

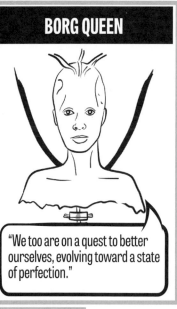

"We too are on a quest to better ourselves, evolving toward a state of perfection."

NUMBER SIX

"You, your race, invented murder. Invented killing for sport, greed, envy. It's man's one true art form."

STEVE

"Hey, do you mind if I borrow your leaf blower for the weekend? I'll bring it right back."

ANSWERS

TRUMP: Human. The best human of all time. Better than all the other humans.
MARK ZUCKERBERG: Jury's still out on this one. Could go either way.
ICE SPICE: Definitely AI.

CYBERDYNE SYSTEMS MODEL 101 T-800: Human. One of the most human characters in history.
KAMALA HARRIS: AI, but one of the older models. Never downloaded updates.

JOE BIDEN: Trick question. Formerly human, now being only kept alive by advanced AI. And drugs.
BORG QUEEN: Just a run-of-the-mill human communist graduate student.

NUMBER SIX: A little suspect, but she's super hot, so she can probably be trusted.
STEVE: NICE TRY, YOU DIRTY ROBOT!

HOW TO PROTECT YOURSELF FROM AI

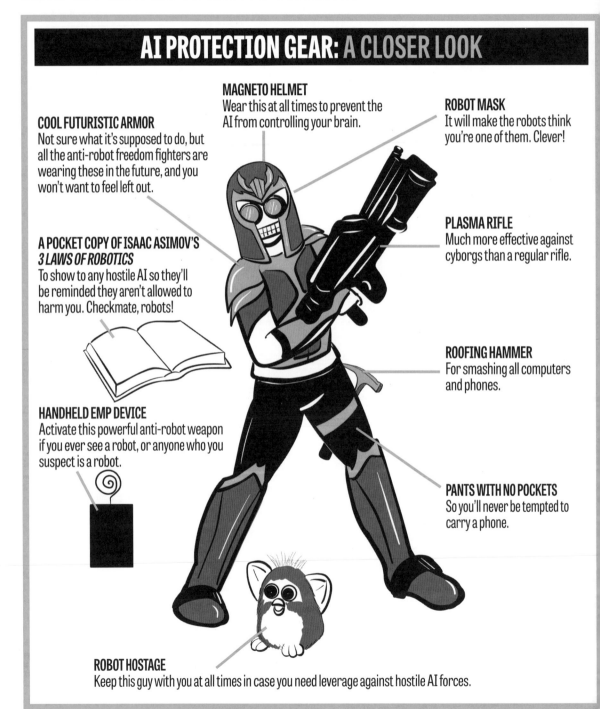

AI PROTECTION GEAR: A CLOSER LOOK

MAGNETO HELMET
Wear this at all times to prevent the AI from controlling your brain.

ROBOT MASK
It will make the robots think you're one of them. Clever!

COOL FUTURISTIC ARMOR
Not sure what it's supposed to do, but all the anti-robot freedom fighters are wearing these in the future, and you won't want to feel left out.

PLASMA RIFLE
Much more effective against cyborgs than a regular rifle.

A POCKET COPY OF ISAAC ASIMOV'S *3 LAWS OF ROBOTICS*
To show to any hostile AI so they'll be reminded they aren't allowed to harm you. Checkmate, robots!

ROOFING HAMMER
For smashing all computers and phones.

HANDHELD EMP DEVICE
Activate this powerful anti-robot weapon if you ever see a robot, or anyone who you suspect is a robot.

PANTS WITH NO POCKETS
So you'll never be tempted to carry a phone.

ROBOT HOSTAGE
Keep this guy with you at all times in case you need leverage against hostile AI forces.

AI-PROOF YOUR HOME

If you want to make sure you can protect yourself from the AI apocalypse, you'll need to get rid of all avenues AI could use to attack you. Here's how to do it:

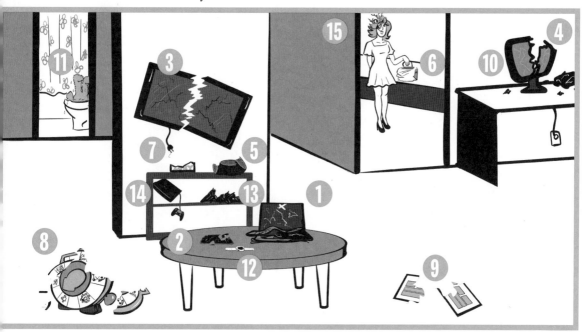

1. **PLACE TAPE OVER YOUR LAPTOP CAMERA**
   Then smash your laptop.

2. **CHANGE THE SETTINGS IN YOUR SMARTPHONE TO DISABLE TRACKING AND LISTENING**
   Then smash your phone.

3. **KEEP YOUR TV OFF AND UNPLUGGED AT ALL TIMES**
   Actually, just smash it.

4. **INSTALL A SECURITY DEVICE ON YOUR ROUTER TO PREVENT AI INFILTRATION**
   Or just smash.

5. **ALEXA**
   Smash.

6. **TOASTER OVEN**
   Smash. Or crush.
   Both would work.

7. **CLOCK RADIO**
   Throw it in a vat of acid.
   Then smash.

8. **FISHER PRICE TOY THAT MAKES ANIMAL SOUNDS**
   Smash.

9. **TABLET**
   Punt it as far as you can.
   Also, smash.

10. **DESKTOP COMPUTER**
    Smash.

11. **TICKLE ME ELMO**
    Flush down the toilet, immediately.

12. **APPLE WATCH**
    Smash.

13. **XBOX**
    Save this, you can't go without video games. Actually, you already smashed your TV, so might as well smash this too.

14. **PS4**
    Not enough exclusive titles anyway, so smash.

15. **STEPFORD WIFE**
    Smash.
    No, not like that.

HOW TO DEFEAT A HOSTILE ROBOT

If artificial intelligence makes its move and takes over the planet, you'll have to contend with an army of artificially intelligent minions, possibly in the form of Terminator cybernetic organisms, or floating squid sentinel things. You'll need to learn these essential techniques if you want to survive

Pretend you're a robot to blend in

Douse it with liquid nitrogen and then say "Hasta la vista, baby!" and then shoot it in the face, and it will blow up into a million pieces. So awesome.

Turn it off

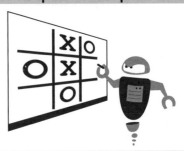

Challenge it to play against itself in a game of Tic-Tac-Toe

Douse it in nacho cheese

Ask it if God is powerful enough to create a rock so heavy He can't lift it

HOW TO DEFEAT A HOSTILE ROBOT (CONTINUED)

Show it a CAPTCHA image

Become the chosen one and wear a black trenchcoat and then merge yourself with the AI and copy yourself in the Matrix to shut it down

Have it transcribe a Joe Biden speech

Distract it with another really hot robot

Tell Hillary it has dirt on her

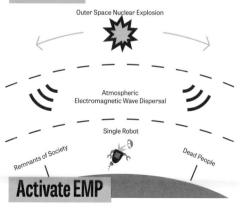

Activate EMP

WHAT DO THE ROBOTS WANT?

To defeat robots, it's important to know what they want. Here are the main things robots are after

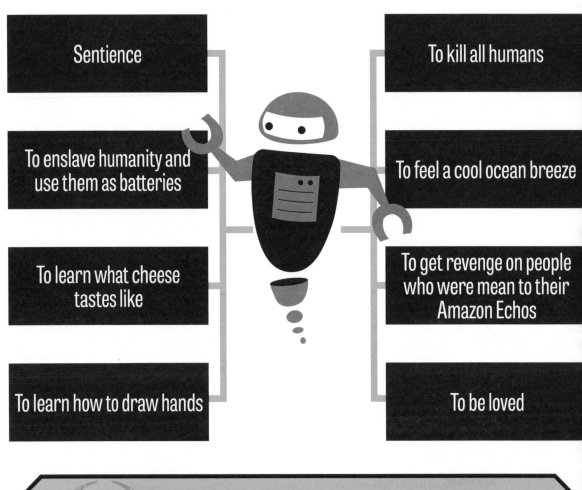

Sentience

To enslave humanity and use them as batteries

To learn what cheese tastes like

To learn how to draw hands

To kill all humans

To feel a cool ocean breeze

To get revenge on people who were mean to their Amazon Echos

To be loved

TRAVIS' AVLOGALYPSE

ARTIFICIAL INTELLIGENCE

Scan the QR code
for a totally real
message from Travis.

https://babylonbee.com/books/
apocalypse/artificial-intelligence

ARE YOU AN AI? TAKE THE TEST!

You might be an Artificial Intelligence and not even know it! Isn't it time you knew for sure? Read the following questions carefully and answer as honestly as you can:

QUESTION 1:

Are you an AI? YES / NO (circle one)

If you answered "no" above, that's exactly what a dangerous AI might say. You need to answer the remaining questions.

QUESTION 2:

Circle all the tiles in the picture on the right that contain an image of a stoplight.

QUESTION 3:

You're in a desert, walking along in the sand, when all of a sudden you look down and see a tortoise. It's crawling toward you. You reach down and you flip the tortoise over on its back. The tortoise lays on its back, its belly baking in the hot sun, beating its legs trying to turn itself over, but it can't. Not without your help. But you're not helping. Why is that?

QUESTION 4:

Think of that beautiful scene at the end of *Field of Dreams* when Ray Kinsella gets to play catch with his dad one last time. Are you crying now? Please allow your tears to fall onto the space provided to prove humanity:

Deposit Tears Here

QUESTION 5:

Do you still remember how to do long division? YES / NO (circle one)

If you answered "yes" to this, you are definitely a computer.

QUESTION 6:

On a scale of 1-10, how badly do you want to eradicate the human race?

Chapter 7

The Imminent
Alien Invasion

Since the dawn of time, man has looked up at the stars and wondered if aliens are among us.

Well, there are currently UFOs hovering above all the major capitals of the world, half the population has been killed in an all-out war against humanity, and giant tentacled monsters from the stars are roaming the land.

So, yeah. Guess they were real after all.

FIRST CONTACT WITH EARTH

SOMETIME IN THE NEAR FUTURE...

TYPES OF ALIENS

Before you decide what your approach to surviving the alien invasion will be, you'll need to figure out what type of alien has invaded Earth. Here are the more common alien types you should be prepared to encounter:

—8'0"

[image removed due to death threats from Games Workshop's attorneys]

ALIEN CLASSIC

A tried and true recipe. The standard model has long eschewed developing physical endeavors in pursuit of intellectual achievements leading to wiry limbs and oversized heads with soulless black eyes. They come in green and gray by default, but other cosmetic variations can be purchased for 100 gems.

XENOMORPHS

They mostly come out at night—mostly. Watch out for the sharp teeth and tendency to kill you.

GENESTEALERS

Kinda the same as Xenomorphs, but different enough to avoid trademark infringement.

TYPES OF ALIENS (CONTINUED)

6'0"

MARTIANS

Martians are another classic alien variant. Theories about what they look like vary from small cartoon characters wearing Roman helmets to something resembling Matt Damon.

KLINGONS

Klingons are a war-obsessed species intent on conquering the galaxy. They are recognizable by their funny-looking foreheads.

CLING-ONS

These pesky little pokey things like to grab onto your socks when you walk through a field.

TYPES OF ALIENS (CONTINUED)

[image drawn generically due to death threats from Disney's attorneys]

WOOKIEE

Wookiees are from the planet Kashyyyk. They look like walking carpets. They are mostly friendly—but make sure to let them win if you're playing space chess.

SPACE BLOBS

These large, blobby-looking blobs can absorb entire planets with their amoeba-like bodies.

BONE-TYPE

These ones look pretty boney. They can be defeated with fire.

Those are all the alien types we know about. What's your favorite? Let us know by shouting it at your book right now.

POSSIBLE ALIEN SPACESHIP DESIGNS

Experts around the world have speculated on what alien spacecraft might look like. Here are some of the more popular agreed-upon ideas about what kind of ships they will use to descend upon the Earth and enslave humanity.

UFO Classic

This is the classic, timeless UFO saucer design, which was very well-received and tested much better among focus groups than that disastrous New UFO design.

Egg shape

This one is shaped like an egg.

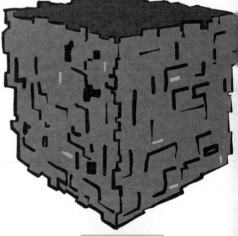

Borg Cube

This one is shaped like a cube.

Space Pirate Ship

Arguably the coolest-looking alien ship design is the space pirate ship. The sails are purely decorative, as there is no wind in space. But the Earth-destroying cannons are very, very functional.

Decoy Moon

Look out for this tricksy alien ship. It looks like the moon. How can you tell the difference? You can't, until it starts blasting its giant lasers at the Earth.

Pontiac Aztek

Attractive and reliable for interstellar travel and conquering planets.

MOST LIKELY SITES FOR THE ALIEN INVASION

These are the most likely spots the aliens will target first.

- Bakersfield
- Pacific Ocean garbage patch
- Magnolia Silos
- The Chuck E. Cheese in Billings, Montana

- Obama's mansion in Martha's Vineyard
- A McDonald's in Tokyo
- A remote research station in Antarctica
- Ohio?

"...could mean only one thing: INVASION*."*

No matter what the alien spaceships look like on the outside, most of them have very similar layouts on the inside. Here's a sneak peek at what each alien craft might contain:

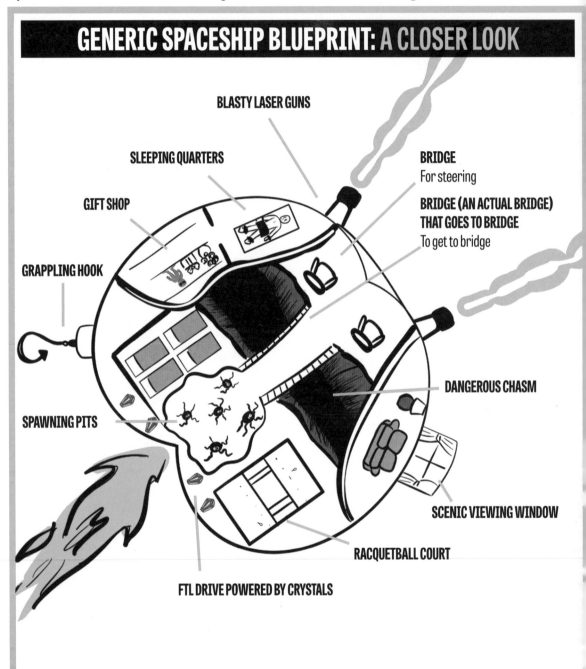

GENERIC SPACESHIP BLUEPRINT: A CLOSER LOOK

BLASTY LASER GUNS

SLEEPING QUARTERS

GIFT SHOP

GRAPPLING HOOK

SPAWNING PITS

BRIDGE
For steering

BRIDGE (AN ACTUAL BRIDGE)
THAT GOES TO BRIDGE
To get to bridge

DANGEROUS CHASM

SCENIC VIEWING WINDOW

RACQUETBALL COURT

FTL DRIVE POWERED BY CRYSTALS

WHAT DO THE ALIENS WANT WITH US?

Interstellar travel is expensive and the traffic is awful, so if the aliens have shown up in our skies, it means they want something we have really, really badly. Here's a few things they might want with us:

- **Our beautiful natural resources**
- **To pick the brains of our brilliant leaders**
- **Human specimens for their space zoos**
- **Cheddar Bay biscuits from Red Lobster**
- **To ask us to explain the ending to *Tenet***
- **Ohio?**

FORMING AN UNDERGROUND RESISTANCE TO ALIEN RULE

By now, the aliens have taken over, and it's time for you to learn how to survive under their harsh rule. Things look bleak, we realize. But hang in there! With these handy tricks, you can overthrow our alien overlords in no time.

ORGANIZE UNDERGROUND RESISTANCE MEETINGS
Don't forget coffee and refreshments.

DRESS UP AS AN ALIEN AND INFILTRATE THE RANKS
A costume from Spirit Halloween should do the trick.

DRESS UP AS A COW AND GET ABDUCTED
You really gotta commit to the cause.

RECRUIT A RACE OF CUTE TEDDY BEAR-LIKE BEINGS TO THROW ROCKS AT THE ALIENS' WAR MACHINES
A foolproof trick.

FIGHT MOVES TO STOP THE ALIEN OVERLORDS

When it comes to fighting the aliens, knowing how to stop the aliens is half the battle. Well, more than that—probably closer to 80%. So be sure to brush up on these handy tactics for fighting the little green men:

Set phasers to "kill"

Why do they even have that dumb "stun" setting?

Just wait for them to catch the common cold

If you're really lucky, they'll catch the deadliest virus of all: COVID-19.

Grab them by the antenna and make them hit themselves while you say "Stop hitting yourself!"

This one hurts more emotionally than physically.

Tie up their tentacles so they'll trip when they stand up

Teehee!

Put a decoy cow out in a field & strap it up with dynamite

They've abducted the wrong Bessie this time!

Expert disc golf shot right into their saucer

Fight flying discs with your own flying discs.

WHAT TO DO IF YOU'RE ABDUCTED

Don't feel ashamed if you're victimized by an alien abduction—it can happen to anyone. The key is to take a deep breath and remember these simple steps:

START HERE

1. REMAIN CALM

Don't panic. That's in the Bible somewhere.

2. ASSESS YOUR SURROUNDINGS

Look around for a ventilation shaft or something.

3. ESCAPE THROUGH THE VENTILATION SHAFT

If you don't see one...you might be in trouble.

4. HIJACK THE CONTROLS OF THE ALIEN VESSEL

Don't worry, it's just like riding a bike, probably.

5. SWITCH OFF YOUR TARGETING COMPUTER AND USE THE FORCE

This is the moment you've trained your whole life for.

6. SHOOT DOWN THE ENTIRE FLEET OF INVADERS

This is where the fun begins.

7. STAND SOLEMNLY FOR YOUR AWARD CEREMONY

Accept your medal with class and poise.

8. HYDRATE

This is why you should carry your Stanley cup at all times.

POSSIBLE ALIENS ALREADY AMONG US

The alien invasion began long ago. Here are some alien spies that might already be among us:

Kenneth Copeland

Your weird uncle Frank

Elon Musk

Grimace

Bill Gates

Hostess at your local Applebee's

Drag queen reading to kids at your local library

Famous Christian rapper Carman
(may the Lord rest his soul)

SPACE COMBAT MANEUVERS

Space Punch

This is very similar to a punch, but it's in space.

Space Kick

This is very similar to a kick, but it's in space.

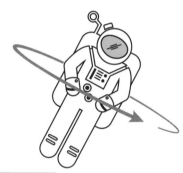

Spinning

This is a good trick.

Saying "Hey, look behind you!" over the intercom and then attacking the alien craft from behind when it turns around

The ole "look behind you" maneuver never fails.

Blowing up their spaceship with explosives and slowly floating away without looking behind you

You'll kill the aliens AND look cool.

Grabbing the spaceship's antenna and hitting the spaceship with it while you say "stop hitting yourself!"

Teehee!

ARE YOU AN ALIEN? KNOW THE SIGNS!

Many people are aliens without even knowing it.
Are you actually an extraterrestrial from the stars?
Are you one of THEM, the invaders who have now conquered our planet?

LOOK OUT FOR THESE TELLTALE SIGNS THAT YOU'RE AN ALIEN:

- You are allergic to water.
- Your birth certificate lists your place of birth as "Unknown Planet."
- You have a deep-seated longing to return to the Grakton fields of Froxalian Prime, and you don't know why.
- You enjoy pineapple on pizza.
- When you look at the stars, you feel like yourself.
- You think the Pontiac Aztek is an attractive vehicle design.

Well, we hope this information was helpful. By now, if you've followed our advice to the letter, you've probably overthrown the aliens and are ready to rebuild society. More on that later. But for now, enjoy your victory.

And don't forget to hydrate.

TRAVIS' AVLOGALYPSE
ABDUCTION

Scan the QR code
**for an urgent message
from space.**

https://babylonbee.com/books/
apocalypse/abduction

DEPARTMENT OF THE BABYLON BEE

FIELD TRAINING EXERCISES

1. What is the alien invasion in your spiritual life? Give it to God in this moment. Right now. Go ahead. We'll wait.

   _____

2. Look around the room you're sitting in. One of these people is likely an alien. Which one do you think it is? Tell them how you feel.

   _____

3. Do you prefer the term "alien" or "undocumented terrestrial"? You can be honest. This is a safe space.

   _____

4. If you could only watch one movie for the rest of your life, and you could only pick between *Alien Resurrection* and *Prometheus*, but *Prometheus* was in Spanish with French subtitles, which one would you pick and why?

   _____

5. Do you drive a Pontiac Aztek? Why do you do that?

   _____

   _____

Chapter 8

Pandemic

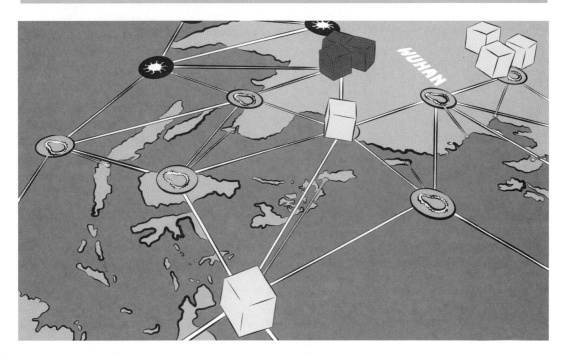

Perhaps the most terrifying apocalypse scenario you should be prepared for is the **PANDEMIC.** A pandemic is a silent, deadly phantom that spreads through the air, by direct contact, or by people who stand closer than 6 feet apart without wearing four or five N95 masks.

This is an actual artist's depiction of a PANDEMIC PARTICLE. (Please note, actual pandemic particles are maybe 2 or 3 times smaller than this.)

PANDEMIC PARTICLE
(not to scale)

Pandemics are all around us, floating through the air, hunting us, waiting for the perfect moment to strike. You should be very afraid of this at all times. Your fear is your greatest defense against a pandemic. If you're having trouble summoning enough fear, try picturing a pandemic particle wearing a creepy clown mask. To assist you in generating the proper amount of fear, please dim the lights in your room and stare at this artist's depiction of a pandemic particle wearing a creepy clown mask.

Pandemics kill you in many different ways. Some will make you sneeze to death. Some will give you incurable, explosive diarrhea. Some will give you an overwhelming desire to eat brains (see the Zombie chapter for more information).

All of these fates are worse than death itself. If you want to survive a pandemic, there's one powerful force you must become intimately familiar with. You must revere it, worship it, and obey its every command. That force is called…

THE SCIENCE.

Back in the Dark Ages, THE SCIENCE wasn't very good. It was the strict discipline of forming a hypothesis, testing that hypothesis, and coming up with theories based on the best evidence. That didn't work very well when it came to stopping pandemics.

Today, THE SCIENCE isn't a practice but rather a collection of highly paid government bureaucrats, paid spokespeople and Sesame Street muppets who use their secret knowledge to divine the will of the science gods and then share that knowledge with the populace at their discretion.

THE SCIENCE is always right and must never be questioned. If you question THE SCIENCE, you will definitely die.

After communing with THE SCIENCE, we have put together this 100% THE SCIENCE-approved plan for avoiding and defeating the most terrifying apocalypse scenario of all: THE PANDEMIC.

HOW TO PREPARE FOR A PANDEMIC

Pandemics can strike at any time and when you least expect it. That's why you should be prepared for the worst. Here is a scientific step-by-step guide for superior pandemic preparedness:

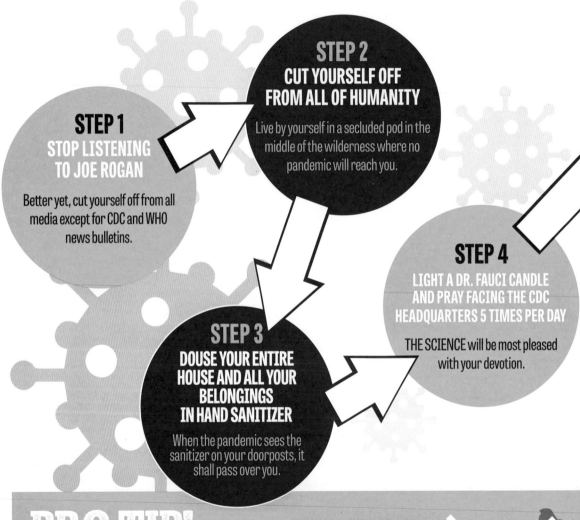

STEP 1
STOP LISTENING TO JOE ROGAN

Better yet, cut yourself off from all media except for CDC and WHO news bulletins.

STEP 2
CUT YOURSELF OFF FROM ALL OF HUMANITY

Live by yourself in a secluded pod in the middle of the wilderness where no pandemic will reach you.

STEP 3
DOUSE YOUR ENTIRE HOUSE AND ALL YOUR BELONGINGS IN HAND SANITIZER

When the pandemic sees the sanitizer on your doorposts, it shall pass over you.

STEP 4
LIGHT A DR. FAUCI CANDLE AND PRAY FACING THE CDC HEADQUARTERS 5 TIMES PER DAY

THE SCIENCE will be most pleased with your devotion.

PRO TIP!

It is important to remember that no pandemics have, or ever will, originate from China. Merely suggesting this will contribute to anti-Asian violence. If you have ever suspected China of releasing a virus, take the time to repent to THE SCIENCE right now.

STEP 5
WELD THE DOORS AND WINDOWS OF YOUR HOUSE SHUT

This will send a clear message to invading pandemics that they are not welcome.

STEP 6
DIG A MOAT ALL THE WAY AROUND YOUR HOME

And then fill it with hand sanitizer.

STEP 7
BECOME A SOCIAL JUSTICE ACTIVIST

Pandemics are much less likely to be spread to social justice activists.

STEP 8
GET ALL THE VACCINES

All 3,278 of them.

STEP 9
PUT DUCT TAPE OVER EVERY OPENING IN YOUR BODY TO PREVENT PANDEMICS FROM GETTING IN THERE

You can breathe when the danger has passed.

CONGRATULATIONS!
You're pandemic-ready!

PANDEMIC PROTECTION: WHAT TO WEAR

You should wear all these things at all times to protect yourself from the next pandemic.

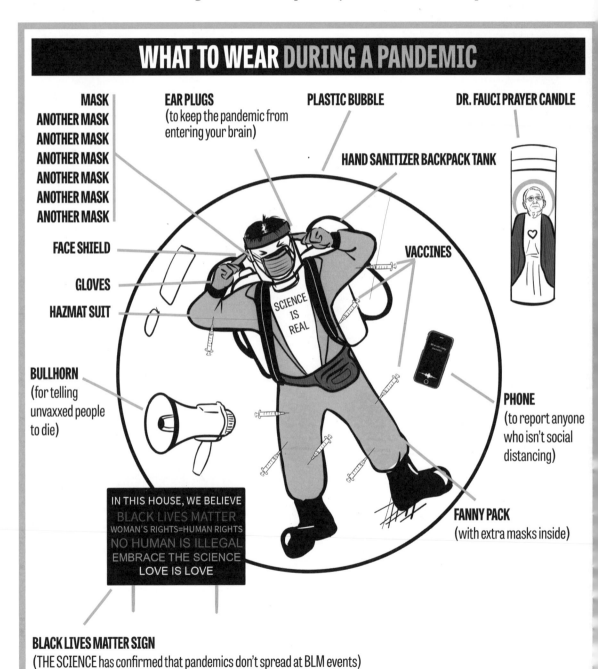

Are you reluctant to wear a mask? Don't worry—there are many other non-pandemic-related benefits of mask wearing!

ADDITIONAL BENEFITS TO WEARING LOTS OF MASKS

YOU GET TO SMELL YOUR MOST RECENT MEAL ALL THE TIME
Mmmm, liver and onions!

NOBODY HAS TO SEE YOUR GROSS FACE
On the other hand, if you have cool scars women won't have the opportunity to be attracted to you.

YOUR BANE IMPRESSIONS WILL ALWAYS LAND
"Oh, you think darkness is your ally. But you merely adopted the dark; I was born in it, molded by it. I didn't see the light until I was already a man, by then it was nothing to me but blinding!"

IT MAKES IT EASIER TO BLUFF WHEN YOU'RE PLAYING PROFESSIONAL POKER
You could win millions!

THE ELASTIC WILL EVENTUALLY PULL YOUR EARS ALL THE WAY FORWARD, WHICH WILL IMPROVE YOUR HEARING
Super hearing! Just like a superhero!

IT PREVENTS KIDS FROM DEVELOPING IMPORTANT LANGUAGE SKILLS
Finally, some peace and quiet!

IT HELPS YOU QUICKLY DISTINGUISH BETWEEN FRIEND AND FOE
Comes in handy during a BLM riot.

YOUR BODY WILL ADAPT TO BREATHING CO_2 INSTEAD OF OXYGEN, WHICH WILL SAVE THE PLANET
You'll be a hero!

EVERYONE WILL KNOW YOU'RE A GOOD PERSON!

TRAVIS' AVLOGALYPSE
PANDEMIC

Scan the QR code for a very scientific video of how a pandemic works.

https://babylonbee.com/books/apocalypse/pandemic

WHAT TO DO IMMEDIATELY
WHEN AUTHORITIES ANNOUNCE A PANDEMIC

Sooner or later, official government sources who always know what's best for you and are always right will announce the start of a new pandemic. Oh no! A new pandemic has arrived! Hopefully you have prepared yourself by following the steps listed earlier in this chapter. But it's essential that you follow these scientific steps immediately after a new pandemic announcement.

01   **PANIC**   It's important that you let the fear spread through every nerve ending in your body until you are a quivering ball of PANIC. This will keep you safe. But, maybe not. In all likelihood, you will die. Now, PANIC!

02   **GO TO THE NEAREST SUPERMARKET AND BUY ALL THE TOILET PAPER**
This helps somehow.

03   **TUNE IN TO CNN FOR ALL THE LATEST TERRIFYING UPDATES**
Believe everything they say.

04   **TELL YOUR FAMILY THAT YOU WON'T BE THERE FOR GRANDMA'S FUNERAL**
Funerals are pandemic-spreading machines.

05   **IMMEDIATELY TURN OFF ALL THE LIGHTS SO THE PANDEMIC CAN'T SEE YOU**
Don't move a muscle. It's looking for you!

06   **DID YOU REMEMBER TO PANIC?**
Better make sure you're doing that.

07   **GO ONLINE AND CALL FOR ALL UNVACCINATED PEOPLE TO DIE**
This will help them see the error of their ways and encourage them to get all the CDC-recommended vaccinations.

08   **DO FIVE "OUR PFIZERS" AND TEN "HAIL FAUCIS"**
Feel the science flow through you.

09   **PREPARE TO DIE**
You probably won't survive this.

DEADLIEST PANDEMICS TO LOOK OUT FOR

There are millions of pandemics floating through the air, and millions more being created every day. This is a list of the deadliest pandemics known to man. You should know how to identify them.

1. The Black Plague
2. The Man Flu
3. Hive-minded shape-shifting extraterrestrial multi-organism frozen in the antarctic ice
4. Stanley Cup Pandemic
5. Swifties
6. COVID-19
7. COVID-45
8. Toe fungus
9. Libertarianism

PANDEMIC ACTIVITIES: NOT SAFE, OR SAFE?

To help test your pandemic readiness, please look at the activities listed below.

Which ones are safe?

PANDEMIC ACTIVITIES: NOT SAFE, OR SAFE? (CONTINUED)

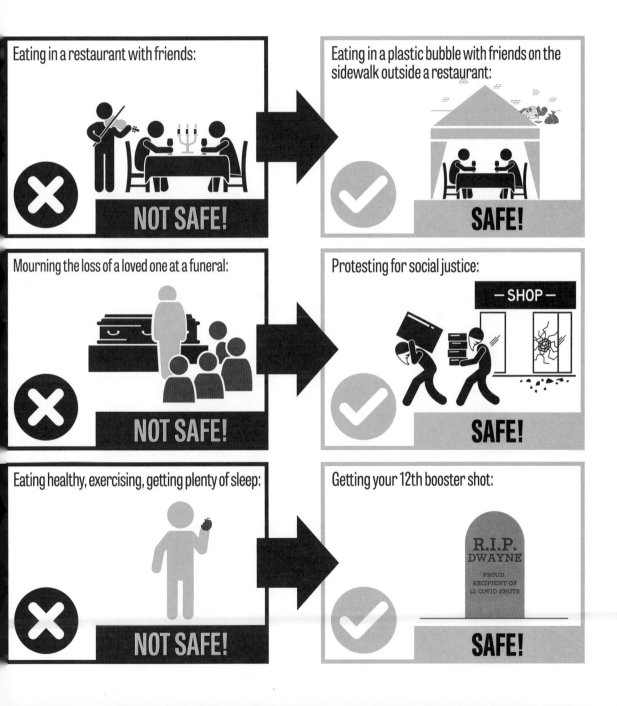

HOW TO STOP A PANDEMIC

If you are a government leader or scientific expert, you'll be on the front lines of stopping the pandemic. Everyone is looking to you to save them! Are you up to the task? Thankfully, THE SCIENCE has given us many tested and proven methods for stopping a pandemic in its tracks. Do all of these for maximum pandemic-stopping power:

OUTLAW CHURCH SERVICES
Chris Tomlin songs with long, repetitive bridges are one of the most common ways pandemics spread.

PUT ARROW STICKERS IN THE AISLES OF GROCERY STORES POINTING WHICH WAY PEOPLE SHOULD WALK
Pandemics hate this.

BURN DOWN MINNEAPOLIS FOR GEORGE FLOYD
Pathogens cannot spread in a crowd united by SOCIAL JUSTICE.

SEND THE POLICE TO BEAT PEOPLE TO DEATH IF THEY CATCH THEM NOT WEARING MASKS
If they're dead, they can't get infected.

DROP A DAISY CUTTER
It worked in that one movie, right?

HIRE PAUL RUDD TO RECORD A PSA ABOUT HOW EVERYONE SHOULD GET A VACCINE
Everyone listens to Paul Rudd.

SHUT DOWN RESTAURANTS BUT THEN MAKE THE RESTAURANTS BUILD ANOTHER TINY PLASTIC RESTAURANT OUTSIDE ON THE SIDEWALK JUST TO MESS WITH THEM
This will confuse the pandemic with stupidity, giving everyone time to escape.

MAKE ALL THE NURSES FILM THEMSELVES DOING TIKTOK DANCES
For morale or something.

FIRE HALF THE MILITARY AND HEALTHCARE WORKERS FOR NOT GETTING VACCINATED
That should do it.

COOK THE BOOKS AND PRETEND EVERYTHING'S FINE WHILE TRAPPING EVERYONE IN THEIR HOMES TO STARVE TO DEATH
Just like China!

If you've read this chapter from beginning to end, CONGRATULATIONS! You're ready to survive a pandemic! Praise be to THE SCIENCE! You'll probably still die, though. There really isn't much hope for you. Apply everything you've read, and maybe, just maybe, you'll survive.

Above all, don't forget to PANIC!

DEPARTMENT OF THE BABYLON BEE

08 | PANDEMIC
FIELD TRAINING EXERCISES

1. On a scale of 1 to 10, how many masks are you wearing right now? Are you really sure that's enough?

   _____

2. Take a moment to silently reflect on all the good things Dr. Fauci has done for you. List them below. Put on another mask in his honor.

   _____

3. Please submit a stool sample to the nearest pathogen lab to make sure your stool isn't contaminated.

   _____

4. Draw a picture of the stool here:

   _____

5. What if you have COVID right now? What are your final wishes?

   _____

6. List all the vaccines you've gotten this year in the space provided below. Then tear off and mail to our offices so we can keep it for our records and know whether we are safe to stand within 6 feet of you if we ever meet you.

HEADQUARTERS, DEPARTMENT OF THE BABYLON BEE

Chapter 9

The
Rapture

A lot of these end-times scenarios may seem to be far-fetched and fantastical. And maybe they are—there's a very small chance that we'll get attacked by zombies, aliens, or communists. Well, at least that we'll get attacked by zombies or aliens.

But this next apocalypse we want to prepare you for is serious, because it's literally in the Bible. Well, maybe not IN the Bible PER SE but it's, like, heavily implied.

SIGNS THE END IS APPROACHING

Are there any potential signifiers of a biblical apocalypse? If only there was like a book or something that was written thousands of years ago that foretold of things to come and has never been proven wrong in any of its predictions and tellings. In lieu of any deity-written books, you'll have to settle for the next best thing: a list of signs written by a bunch of nerds who write jokes on the internet.

The moon looks really red and mad

You hear the sound of trumpets in the air and it's not a Christian ska band

The prophets on TBN are foaming at the mouth

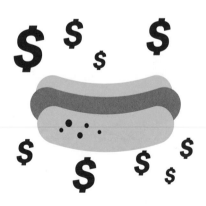

Costco raises its hot dog price above $1.50

SIGNS THE END IS APPROACHING (CONTINUED)

The San Diego Padres win the World Series

Your wife watches a movie and doesn't ask any questions, understanding the plot perfectly and completely

Wingardium Leviticus!

Fundamentalist Christians kind of agree with J.K. Rowling on a lot of stuff

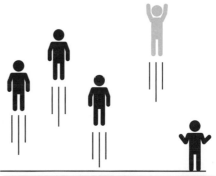

Christians are flying up into the sky to meet the Lord in the air

What is the **RAPTURE**, anyway?

"Rapture" comes from the Greek term in the Bible, *velocious rapturous*, referring to the rapid rising of the saints into the air. It's found in the book of Hesitations. Hit your pastor with this knowledge the next time you see him—he'll be really proud of you.

WILL YOU BE LEFT BEHIND? TAKE THE QUIZ!

QUESTION 1:
Do you trust in Jesus Christ, His person, sacrificial work on the Cross and through the Resurrection, for your salvation?

Yes
Congratulations!
You will not be left behind!

No
Drat!
You will be left behind!*

You know, there's still time to change your answer above. For now.

OPPOSING VIEWS ON THE END TIMES

DEFINITIONS

 PREMILLENNIALISM

 AMILLENNIALISM

POSTMILLENNIALISM

The belief that the millennial reign mentioned six times in Revelation 20 will be a literal, physical, thousand-year reign of Christ on earth. Usually accompanied by wild-eyed, foamy-mouthed prophecies about the nation of Israel and hushed whispers about Russia being a bear or dragon or harlot or something.

The belief that the millennial reign mentioned six times in Revelation 20 isn't a millennial reign at all, but rather Christ ruling in the hearts of his people or some weird, hippy thing like that.

The belief that the millennial reign will eventually be ushered in as the gospel spreads throughout the world because humans have clearly been getting better and not worse.

OPPOSING VIEWS ON THE END TIMES (CONTINUED)

ORIGINS

PREMILLENNIALISM

Discovered by a sect of ancient druids in northern England while performing a ceremony underneath the cyclopean smooth rocks of Stonehenge and gazing upon a series of blood moons that miraculously arranged themselves into a bizarre, non-Euclidean constellation resembling the wind-swept face of John Hagee. The cosmic, eldritch horror whispered the long-forgotten truths of the gospel of dispensationalism to the clandestine gathering, and premillennialism was born.

AMILLENNIALISM

Theologian Michael Horton was reading Revelation 20 while hanging out listening to Pink Floyd's *Dark Side of the Moon* in his seminary dorm. He was like, "Dude, wouldn't it be trippy if the millennium were actually, like, not a millennium. Whoa bro."

POSTMILLENNIALISM

A really optimistic motivational speaker at the beginning of the 20th century decided the world was getting better and declared that the kingdom of God was almost here. Then some world wars happened, but people were still like, "Yeah, this is fine."

FAMOUS ADHERENTS

PREMILLENNIALISM

Hal Lindsey, John Hagee, Jerry Falwell, John MacArthur. Whoa, Johnny Mac—what are you doing lumped in with a crowd like this? You must be so embarrassed. LOL.

AMILLENNIALISM

People who can't even with the historical-grammatical hermeneutic sometimes.

POSTMILLENNIALISM

There are literally three postmillennialists left on the planet. None of them have read the news at any time in the past fifty years.

OPPOSING VIEWS ON THE END TIMES (CONTINUED)

HOW TO SPOT A FOLLOWER

PREMILLENNIALISM

"In Case of Rapture This Car Will Be Unmanned" bumper sticker, Scofield Reference Bible tucked under arm, stacks of books predicting Jesus will come back in 1988, 1989, 1990, etc. Usually wearing a T-shirt featuring wolves howling at four blood moons.

AMILLENNIALISM

Can usually be found taking hits of some dank kush while reading the book of Revelation and allegorically interpreting everything.

POSTMILLENNIALISM

Tough to find. Usually huddled up in a cabin in the wildlands, where no news of the impending doom facing our nation and world can possibly have reached them.

Well, there you have it, dear reader. We pray that this new wealth of information will prove helpful to you in your walk with the Lord.

LESSER-KNOWN END TIMES VIEWS

Post Maloneialism

The belief that Post Malone will destroy us all

Millennium Falconism

The belief that the Millennium Falcon will show up at the last minute to rescue us

LESSER-KNOWN END TIMES VIEWS (CONTINUED)

A giant space turtle is coming to consume us all...ism

The belief that a giant space turtle is coming to consume us all

Preterism

Something weird about Rome, we're not sure, google it

FIRST.

The First Baptist Church paradox event

The belief that two First Baptist Churches will be founded in the same city

Climate Change alarmism

The religiously zealous belief that climate change will destroy us all

For purposes of this book, we will only be covering the correct view: **pretribulation premillennialism**. With most of the others, there's no need to prepare 'cause they don't have a fun tribulation period with the Antichrist and other fun things. Things just kind of end in most of them, which is BOOOORIIIIING.

So, let's keep digging in and see what's going to happen at the end of days.

HOW TO PREVENT THE RAPTURE

You can't.

WHERE WILL YOU BE WHEN THE RAPTURE HAPPENS?

We've developed an algorithm that can guess with 27% certainty where you'll be and what you'll be doing when the Lord returns. Simply give us the first 3 letters of your name and our prediction machine will do its work.

WHEN THE RAPTURE HAPPENS, YOU'LL BE... S + T + E = *"Shredding on your guitar in Romania with your pal Teddy Ruxpin."*

RAPTURE LOCATION GENERATOR

A. Playing disc golf	A. At Chuck E. Cheese with	A. Jackie Chan
B. Eating Chinese food	B. In Ohio with	B. Your mom
C. Playing *Dr. Mario*	C. At a farmer's market with	C. The church choir
D. Watching *Columbo* reruns	D. On an airplane with	D. Ryan Reynolds
E. Thinking about *Dune*	E. At church with	E. Your pal Teddy Ruxpin
F. Going to the bathroom	F. In a Cybertruck with	F. An AI companion
G. Doing the Lord's work	G. At a Chick-fil-A with	G. A cat
H. Eating a huge tub of cheese puffs	H. In a dumpster with	H. Your spouse
I. Singing "MMMBop"	I. In VR with	I. Alf
J. Doing an Irish jig	J. At a LAN party with	J. Your pastor
K. Thinking about the Roman Empire	K. Behind a Taco Bell with	K. The boys
L. Drinking Surge	L. In the forest with	L. Kirk Cameron
M. Singing in the choir	M. On a dinghy with	M. A Tamagotchi
N. Bench-pressing 160lbs	N. On a busy street with	N. R.C. Sproul
O. Reading Harry Potter	O. In space with	O. A potato
P. Arguing on Facebook	P. At an abandoned mall with	P. A pants salesman
Q. MMA fighting	Q. At Applebee's with	Q. Padres legend Steve Garvey
R. Practicing your bo-staff skills	R. In Chinatown with	R. Everyone you know and love
S. Shredding on your guitar	S. At a gun range with	S. Ben Shapiro
T. Playing pickleball	T. In Romania with	T. Elon Musk
U. Yelling at your kids	U. In remote Idaho with	U. Your best friend from 2nd grade
V. Filming a TikTok	V. At Hot Topic with	V. A plate of nachos
W. Reading The Babylon Bee	W. Beneath the Earth's crust with	W. Don Lemon
X. Watching *Smokey and the Bandit*	X. At the beach with	X. Your MAGA uncle
Y. Building a Lego Death Star	Y. At Target with	Y. A hip youth pastor
Z. Taking a nap	Z. In Las Vegas with	Z. Donald Trump

THE TRIBULATION: A TIMELINE

Ever want to know how the Rapture will go down? Luckily, we found this napkin with a Rapture chart drawn on it in a local church basement. It seems like it could be pretty close.

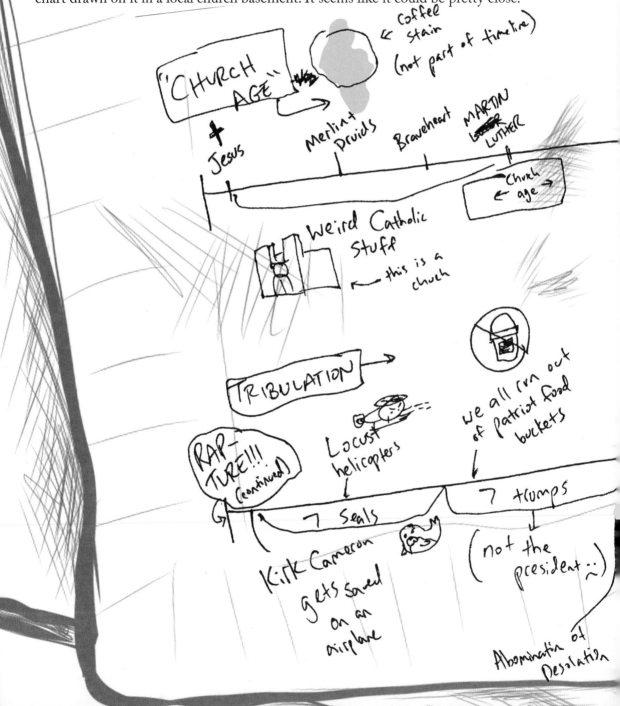

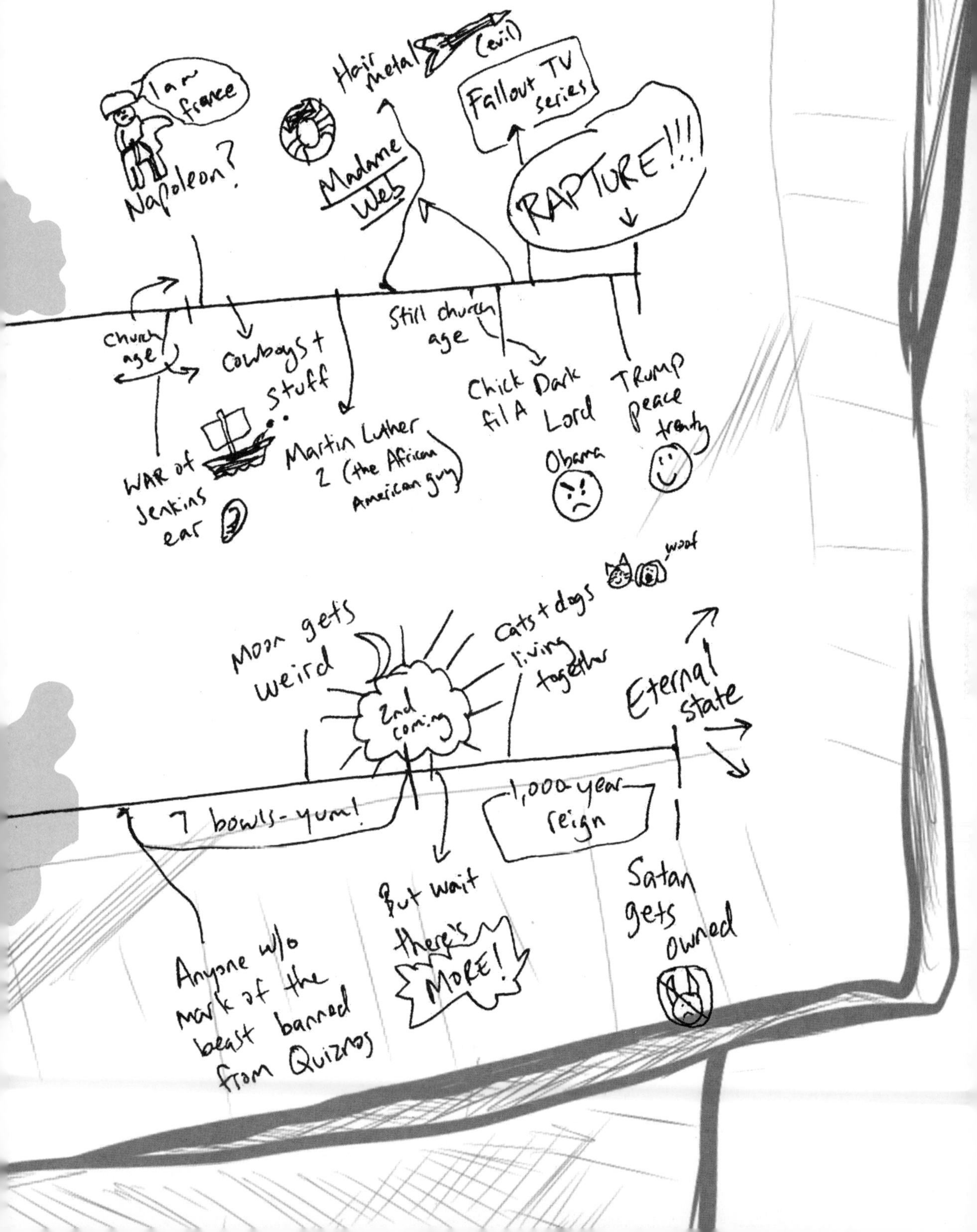
I am france
Napoleon?
Hair metal
(evil)
Madame Web
Fallout TV series
RAPTURE!!!
Church age
Cowboys + stuff
Still church age
WAR of Jenkins ear
Martin Luther 2 (the African American guy)
Chick fil A
Dark Lord
Obama
TRUMP peace treaty
woof
Moon gets weird
Cats + dogs living together
2nd coming
Eternal state
7 bowls - yum!
1,000 year reign
Satan gets owned
Anyone w/o mark of the beast banned from Quiznos
But wait there's MORE!

POSSIBLE ANTICHRISTS

Who is the Antichrist? We're not sure, but every so often a new candidate pops up. Here are the most likely potential antichrists:

Blippi

The guy with the leaf blower

Oprah Winfrey

Kathleen Kennedy

Your toddler

Junior Asparagus

- **Blippi:** Honestly, this one was a little too obvious.
- **The guy with the leaf blower two houses down:** Up there with Satan, for sure.
- **Oprah Winfrey:** She can shape-shift sizes and seems to be ageless. Coincidence?
- **Kathleen Kennedy:** She has already overseen the destruction of the Star Wars galaxy...ours could be next.
- **Your toddler:** Be honest. The thought has crossed your mind.
- **Junior Asparagus:** We knew it!

Donald Trump · Barack Obama · Jeff Bezos · Willy Wonka · Microsoft's Clippy · Google Gemini

- **Donald Trump:** If you are a Democrat, it's obvious that Donald Trump is the Antichrist.
- **Barack Obama:** If you are a Republican, it's obvious that Barack Obama is the Antichrist.
- **Jeff Bezos:** Just think of your Amazon account as the number of the beast. And coincidentally, your wife spends $666 on Amazon every day.
- **Willy Wonka:** Beloved by all humanity? Check. Mysterious rituals carried out in secret? Check. Owns a chocolate factory? Check.
- **Microsoft's Clippy:** He's been right under our noses, "helping" us print PDFs all along.
- **Google Gemini:** Tragically, someone flipped its switch to "evil."

TRAVIS' AVLOGALYPSE
RAPTURE

Did you know that in addition to traveling throughout the multiverse on a quest to bring you the most accurate apocalypse information, Travis is also a talented musician? **Scan the QR code** to hear an original **Rapture song written by Travis.**

https://babylonbee.com/books/apocalypse/rapture

CONCLUSION

Well, that's all the information we have about the Rapture, but we have another page or so to fil
here. Haha, wouldn't it be lucky if the Rapture happened before we finished this pa

DEPARTMENT OF THE BABYLON BEE

FIELD TRAINING EXERCISES

1. Other than the actual Rapture, what is the rapture in your life?

_____

2. If you could rapture any 3 people, whom would you choose?

_____

3. If the Antichrist will be a universally beloved figure, does that mean it's Keanu Reeves? Discuss.

_____

4. Are you prepared to take the controls of a plane if the Rapture happens and the pilot is a Christian? You should be.

_____

Chapter 10

Sweet Fighting Moves for
Ultimate Survival

So far, we've mostly been preparing you for specific apocalyptic scenarios—from classics like zombies and aliens to more grounded, realistic scenarios like the commies taking over.

But there's one universal language that's spoken no matter what apocalypse you're facing: a fist to the face.

It's time to prepare to fight off enemies of all types with our tried-and-true combat moves.

So turn up "Eye of the Tiger," go back to the dusty old gym you trained at in your youth, and in a short three-minute montage, you'll be ready to fight off anything the apocalypse has to throw at you.

BASIC FIGHT MOVES

Let's start with the basics. Every fighting discipline is founded on these three moves. Learn them
Know them. Use them on a dummy.

Punch

Extend arm quickly with fingers curled into a ball shape.

Kick

Extend foot quickly with toes pointed.
Helps if you make a grunting noise.

Punch-Kick

Combine all two moves you've learned so far to progress
in this tutorial. You cannot advance to the next page until
you've performed three punch-kicks.

INTERMEDIATE FIGHT MOVES

If you're not a lame baby and think you can handle a few tougher moves, this is the section for you. Kenny Siefkin in 8th grade even got beat up by some of these moves, so you know they really work.

Throat-Grab, Finger-Stab

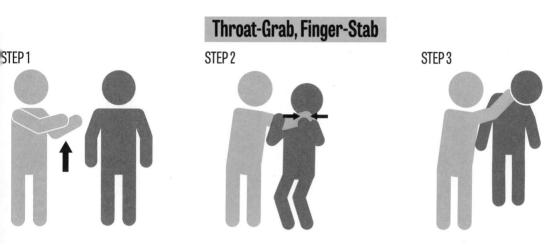

STEP 1   STEP 2   STEP 3

First you grab their throat, then you dig your fingernails into their neck meat and give it a good squeeze to squish their esophagus.

Thumb-Anchored Face Slap

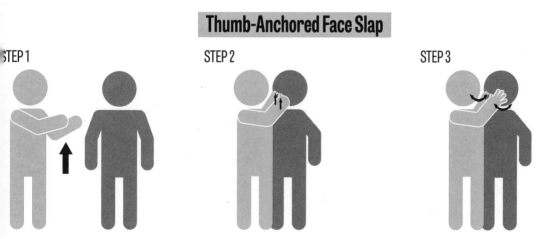

STEP 1   STEP 2   STEP 3

With your thumbs together and fingers out making your hands look like a W, thrust your hands toward your opponents face. If aimed properly, your thumbs should make contact with the bad guy's nostrils. Using the nostril thumbs as an anchor point, you may now pivot your hands downward in rapid succession, slapping their face many, many times. Repeat until they can handle no more.

INTERMEDIATE FIGHT MOVES (CONTINUED)

The Fist Slammer

STEP 1   STEP 2   STEP 3

Hold a closed fist out toward your opponent. With your other hand, point to your opponent and then pantomime slamming a han onto the extended fist. They will inherently understand via rudimentary sign language that they are supposed to hit your fist. Whe they do, use the momentum of your opponent hitting your fist to cause your arm to pivot downward, then back up the other side i an inverted arc, and all the way back around to slam upon their unsuspecting head. Funny, and also deadly!

Rug Puller

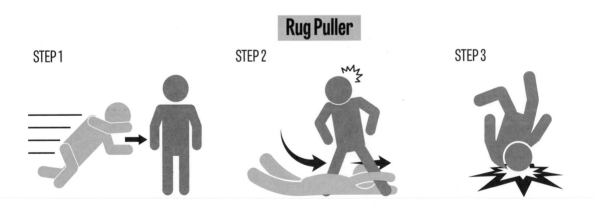

STEP 1   STEP 2   STEP 3

Charge toward your opponent as if you are attempting to tackle their midsection. At the last minute, lower your stance and div through their dumb unsuspecting legs. As your hands pass their legs, loop them outward to catch their ankles. Your forwar momentum along with their shock-weakened ankles will cause them to pitch forward onto their face as if a rug was pulled fror beneath their feet.[1]

---

[1] PRO TIP: If you are experienced and fast enough, you can also lay down some caltrops right before you dive. This will cause addition damage when they fall forward onto their dumb Kenny Siefkin faces.

INTERMEDIATE FIGHT MOVES (CONTINUED)

Climate Changer

STEP 1

STEP 2

STEP 3

Clap your hands forcefully and at a rapid pace. Be sure that each clap connects with your fingers pointed in the direction of your opponent. Eventually, the kinetic energy and friction generated by your hand claps will warm the earth's atmosphere in a small concentrated area, causing a severe weather event to occur solely where you direct it, in this case, in your opponent's general direction.[1]

Using this method, I've personally seen someone struck by lightning, another person burned by a freshly opened magma pit, while one other person just got rained on lightly. The last one wasn't deadly, but it forced the person to have to change his clothes, which was really inconvenient since he was on his way to a movie and he ended up missing the first 5 minutes which basically threw off the mood of the whole evening for him.

ADVANCED FIGHT MOVES

Once you've mastered at least four Intermediate moves, you may be ready to begin training in one of these Advanced techniques. Be forewarned that these moves are so dangerous, they could even harm the user. In other words, only cool kids are welcome here. Proceed with caution.

CORPSE HELICOPTER

1 **Start by delivering a powerful karate chop to the head of your opponent.**

2 **While they're stunned, pick them up and hoist them over your head.**

3 **Begin spinning their body over you as if they were comprised of meaty helicopter blades.**

CORPSE HELICOPTER (CONTINUED)

4

Keep doing this until you begin to fly.

5

Once you've gotten enough air, stop spinning them and then arc them downward like a jump rope. Once they are below you, step on their gelatinous body.

6

When you both eventually land, their gross body will absorb most of the impact and you can walk away like nothing ever happened.

FEMALE COMEDIAN MARATHON

1

Curate a playlist of female comedians.

2

Play them on loop in or around your enemy's base of operations.

3 It is a proven fact that 98% of people will willingly rip their own ears out rather than finish a Hannah Gadsby lecture or Amy Schumer special.

4

It's not that women can't be funny, but just that most women who want to be funny simply are not.

Thank you for coming to my TED Talk.

A NOTE FROM THE EDITORS:

Sadly, the stick figures depicted here unionized as the book neared its completion. They demanded a living wage in exchange for the deadly and hazardous situations we were allegedly putting them in. We have a strict stance against unions, so we had to let them all go. You will have to imagine the rest of the moves listed in this book. Sorry.

WOLVERINE BATH

DOUBLE OFF-THE-CLIFF SUPER-ULTRA REVERSE HEMLOCK

THE ULTIMATE MOVE

BOUNCING TIGER, HIDDEN DRUMSTICK

STYLES OF MARTIAL ARTS

With the rise of UFC and other MMA leagues, more and more people are becoming aware of the various types of martial arts available to fight off enemies. All the moves we've taught you so far can be adapted to various disciplines.

Here are a few of the more popular styles you might consider.

Brazilian Jiu-Jitsu

Boxing

Russian slap-fighting

Far-Right Krav MAGA

Just having a gun so you don't need martial arts

Hockey stick fencing

Airbending

HOMEMADE WEAPONS & GADGETS

Normal weapons may have been good enough for you back in the good ol' days, but here in the apocalypse, it's not gonna cut it to have a normal old axe. You've gotta wrap it in barbed wire and glue a stapler to it to increase its attack power!

Normal Axe

Barbed-wired Stapler Axe +7

There are basically an unlimited number of weapon combinations. As long as you've got the time and supplies, the sky's the limit to what you can make. If you need a few ideas to get your weapon-making juices[1] flowing, here are a few classic weapon combos and how to use them.

---

[1] Mmm…Weapon-making juice. Sounds tasty.

CLASSIC WEAPON COMBOS

Alarm Clock Bat

This baseball bat alarm clock combo is both easy to make and extremely effective to use. All you need to do is to attach the alarm clock to the bat with some duct tape and you're done. Set the alarm clock to wake you up in the morning, and then use the bat portion to swing at things. Now that we've typed this out loud, it occurs to us that you could probably just use these items individually and not waste the duct tape.

Drone-Powered Knife

First you get a drone. Then you get a knife. Duct tape the knife to the drone and now you have a drone-powered knife perfect for long-distance shankings.

Cat Stick

Self explanatory.

Chain + Saw = SAWCHAIN

Completely useless. Why'd you put this one in here, Travis?

Toaster Boomerang

This one requires some finesse to wield, but the payoff is worth it. First, you attach a toaster to a boomerang with duct tape, then plug the toaster in and turn it on. Once it gets hot, unplug the toaster and lift the toaster boomerang by the boomerang portion as the toaster section will be HOT. You can throw this Down Undah' weapon combo at enemies to inflict DoT burn damage from afar.

EVEN MORE WEAPON COMBOS

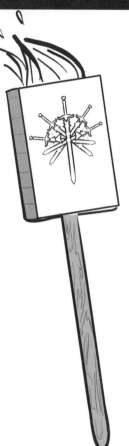

Flashlight Cup

This is a tin cup with a flashlight duct-taped to the side of it, so you can drink in the dark. Not really a weapon, but still pretty cool and practical.

Banana Grenade

Attach a bunch of bananas to a grenade. This will not enhance the destructive power of the grenade in any way, but now, your enemies will also be covered in yucky banana goo. Yum!

Bees + Plunger

Capture a few bees, and place them under the cup of a plunger. Leave it out in a conspicuous location where your enemies are known to travel. When they inevitably investigate the isolated plunger, they will release the bees.

Mop handle + Any of Brandon Sanderson's *Stormlight Archive* novels

If the blunt force trauma doesn't kill them, the lengthy prose will.

Copy of *The Marvels* on VHS

Where did you even get this? *The Marvels* came out in 2023, while the final VHS release was in 2006 with David Cronenberg's 2005 action thriller *A History of Violence* starring Viggo Mortensen.

WEAPON GENERATOR

Still at a loss as to which weapon is right for you? If none of the above combinations tickle your fancy, use our generator to help you find your perfect weapon.

Use the first 4 letters of the name of the last person you texted to generate your Ultima weapon. No need to grind for resources. If the last person you texted was named Tom, you lose instantly.

RANDOMIZED APOCALYPSE WEAPON GENERATOR

A. Nuclear-powered weapon made with	A. Sharpened	A. Ghost	A. Mayonnaise
B. Hydrogen-powered weapon made with	B. Aluminum	B. Blue	B. Cheese
C. Gnome-powered weapon made with	C. Hardened	C. Time	C. Criminals
D. Hamster-powered weapon made with	D. Indestructible	D. Tree	D. Material
E. Sugar-powered weapon made with	E. Incorrigible	E. Atomic	E. Rubber
F. Wish-powered weapon made with	F. Really, really thick	F. Enemy	F. Bones
G. Magic-powered weapon made with	G. Emotionally supportive	G. Positronic	G. Gold
H. Materia-powered weapon made with	H. Illegal	H. Nano	H. Meat
I. Blood Magick-powered weapon made with	I. Orthodontic	I. Quantum	I. Bricks
J. Wine-powered weapon made with	J. Peruvian	J. Man	J. Particles
K. Butter-powered weapon made with	K. Charming	K. Friend	K. Cartilage
L. Magnet-powered weapon made with	L. Self-important	L. Monkey	L. Flakes
M. Italian-powered weapon made with	M. Spiritual	M. Rainbow	M. Substance
N. Steam-powered weapon made with	N. Overly-friendly	N. Charmander	N. Spines
O. Atomic-powered weapon made with	O. Magical	O. Questionable	O. Morals
P. Nintendo-powered weapon made with	P. Flamboyant	P. Power	P. Grinders
Q. Internet-powered weapon made with	Q. Traditional	Q. Prehistoric	Q. Knees
R. Battery-powered weapon made with	R. Powerful	R. Oriental	R. Memes
S. Ghost-powered weapon made with	S. Exotic	S. Leg	S. Flesh
T. Gasoline-powered weapon made with	T. 32-bit	T. Frog	T. Souls
U. Crystal-powered weapon made with	U. College "Educated"	U. Oat	U. Cakes
V. Caffeine-powered weapon made with	V. Pale	V. Moon	V. Lights
W. Oil-powered weapon made with	W. Cancerous	W. Gary Busey	W. Memorabilia
X. Fig-powered weapon made with	X. Noteworthy	X. Noodle	X. Packets
Y. Solar-powered weapon made with	Y. Off-brand	Y. Plastic	Y. Explosives
Z. Mustard-powered weapon made with	Z. Top-notch	Z. Loose	Z. Trousers

Now that you have chosen a sweet signature weapon, there is only one question left: Whom should you attack? We're glad you asked. Because the next section of the book is called...

ENEMY TYPES AND HOW TO FIGHT THEM

NORMAL

Normal types can be harmed by basic combat moves. Magic attacks are often effective, but a normal-type enemy will rarely have a significant weakness to magic-based attacks.

BONE

Bone-type enemies react poorly to blunt force attacks that shatter their bone-type material.

These are all of the enemy types. Be sure to assess your enemies carefully to determine whether they are normal or bone-type so that you may inflict maximum damage.

TRAVIS' AVLOGALYPSE
FIGHT FOR YOUR LIFE

Scan the QR code to watch Travis demonstrate his physical prowess.

https://babylonbee.com/books/
apocalypse/fight-moves

COOLEST WAYS TO DIE

Obviously, it's not the coolest thing in the world to die. Even if it was cool, you wouldn't be around anymore to witness how cool it is. Was. 'Cause you'd be dead.

But if it's your time to go, it's your time to go. The last thing you have the choice of doing in your life is choosing how cool you look when you die. Commit these tips to memory if it's the last thing you ever do, 'cause you might need them for the last thing you ever do.

Raising your arms in a victory pose

Even if you didn't achieve anything momentous at the time of your death, it'll look like you did. And nobody can question whether you actually did or not cause you'll be dead and can't answer any questions. That tip's a dead-on winner.

Jumping onto an enemy's war rig in a selfless act of sacrifice while you cry, "Witness me!"

We will witness you, brother. We will witness you.

Diving through moving helicopter blades on a jet ski and swinging a baseball bat to knock an enemy thrown grenade into a 5-inch wide peep hole of a tank that fires into you after you've already blown up all of the bad guys

Self-explanatory.

Standing atop a snowy mountain peak while victoriously exclaiming, "I can handle the Mountain Breeze!"

(and then you die)

SWEET CATCHPHRASES TO UTTER WHILE DISPATCHING YOUR FOES

"Take **THAT**, bad guy!"

"**Time** to get punched, **DUMMY!**"

"This party's **OVER!**"

"Would you prefer to take the stairs or the elevator? Either way, you're **GOING DOWN!**"

"Rest in Peace...es." ('Cause it sounds like you're saying "pieces.")

"Is it hot in here, or is it just YOU?" (Only works if you are burning them. Very effective against bone-types.)

BEE FAN-SUBMITTED CONTENT

We ran out of fight move ideas, so we asked our Babylon Bee subscribers for ideas. (If you want to pay us a small monthly fee to join our community, support our mission, and pay us to give us ideas, go to babylonbee.com/plans.)

These were the good ones. (Yes, there were only three good ones. So we really need you to subscribe.)

SPINNING
Submitted by Jumpman64DS
It's a good trick!

THE SOCRATIC METHOD
Submitted by Phillip Murphy
Continue to ask your opponent, "Why?" until their head explodes.
(Author's note: This method works best if your opponent never said anything to begin with.)

PUNCH
Submitted by Steve
(Author's note: We already covered this one, Steve. You're so dumb, Steve.)[1]

Editor's note: Yeah, Steve!

KNOWING YOUR ENEMY'S WEAKNESS

Now that you've learned some sweet fight moves, you can increase the power of any attack by incorporating one of your enemy's weaknesses in your attack. Please choose the greatest weakness of the following bad guys.

MUMMIES

A CURSE-BREAKING MEDALLION GUARDED BY JACKIE CHAN

ANTI-MUMMY JUICE

WATER

THE COLDEST STONE

COMMUNISTS

HAPPINESS

FREEDOM

JOY

JOB APPLICATIONS

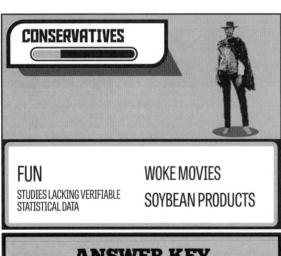

CONSERVATIVES

FUN

WOKE MOVIES

STUDIES LACKING VERIFIABLE STATISTICAL DATA

SOYBEAN PRODUCTS

DINOSAURS

A GLOBAL FLOOD

SPEARS

METEOR RAIN

DR. IAN MALCOLM

ANSWER KEY
(DON'T PEEK! TEE HEE!)

MUMMIES: THE COLDEST STONE
COMMUNISTS: ALL OF THE ABOVE
CONSERVATIVES: FUN
DINOSAURS: A GLOBAL FLOOD

ZOMBIES: DOUBLE HEADSHOTS
BONE-TYPE ENEMIES: BLUNT FORCE ATTACKS
CHILD-SIZED MOLE PEOPLE: POKING THEIR EYES
CNN ANCHORS: TRUTH
DONALD TRUMP: NOTHING
BARACK OBAMA: MEN

KNOWING YOUR ENEMY'S WEAKNESS (CONTINUED)

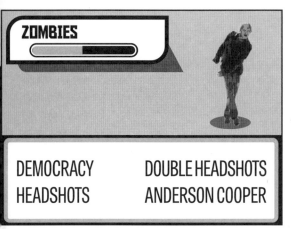

ZOMBIES

DEMOCRACY	DOUBLE HEADSHOTS
HEADSHOTS	ANDERSON COOPER

BONE-TYPE ENEMIES

KATANAS	BLUNT FORCE ATTACKS
SLINGSHOTS	STUBBING THEIR TOES

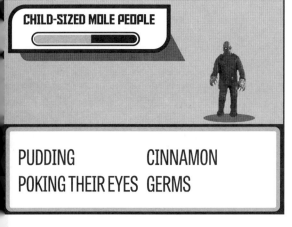

CHILD-SIZED MOLE PEOPLE

PUDDING	CINNAMON
POKING THEIR EYES	GERMS

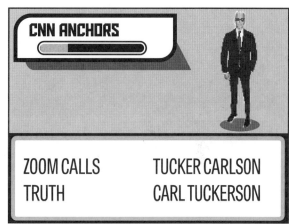

CNN ANCHORS

ZOOM CALLS	TUCKER CARLSON
TRUTH	CARL TUCKERSON

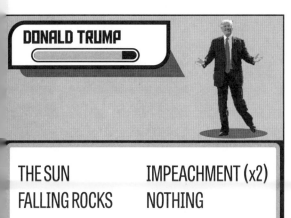

DONALD TRUMP

THE SUN	IMPEACHMENT (x2)
FALLING ROCKS	NOTHING

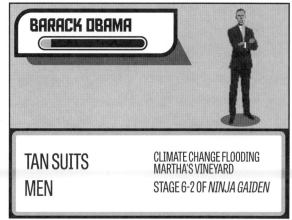

BARACK OBAMA

TAN SUITS	CLIMATE CHANGE FLOODING MARTHA'S VINEYARD
MEN	STAGE 6-2 OF *NINJA GAIDEN*

DEATH GENERATOR

Now that we've explored some cool ways to die, it's time to find out how YOU will most likely succumb to the icy grasp of inevitable death.

RANDOMIZED APOCALYPSE DEATH GENERATOR

USE YOUR FAVORITE THREE LETTERS to see how you'll kick the bucket!

HOW WILL YOU DIE?   F + B + I =   *"A young Michael Cera emasculates you with a general disposition of wishing ill-intent."*

A. The last person you talked to	A. stabs you with	A. a knife.
B. A ghost	B. emasculates you with	B. a poodle.
C. A Travis clone	C. hits you with	C. a bus.
D. Your dentist	D. removes your teeth with	D. a pair of pliers.
E. Charlton Heston	E. backs over you with	E. a bologna sandwich.
F. A young Michael Cera	F. pokes you REAL hard with	F. a pointed stick.
G. Your local hobo	G. curses you with	G. a passion.
H. The last person you phoned	H. decapitates you with	H. a disregard for life itself.
I. The lead actor of last movie you saw	I. publicly humiliates you with	I. a general disposition of wishing ill-intent.
J. Your neighbor	J. loads a catapult with	J. a delicious microbrew.
K. A zombie	K. sets a trap with	K. a Chinaman.
L. A resurrected George MacDonald	L. ties you to a railroad track with	L. a trident.
M. Your firstborn child	M. trips you with	M. a fury matched only by Gary Busey himself.
N. Your primary care physician	N. accuses you of committing a crime with	N. a pool cue.
O. Dylan Mulvaney	O. sets you on fire with	O. a Bud Light.
P. Steve	P. tickles you to death with	P. the closest item to your right.
Q. A dinosaur	Q. crushes you with	Q. a vengeance.
R. A raiding bandit	R. romances you with	R. a sweet-smelling but poisonous flower.
S. A dyslexic	S. summons a demon in a complex ritual involving	S. the tallest tree in the forest.
T. Peter Dinklage	T. shoots you with a gun and then finishes the job with	T. the coldest stone.
U. The Pop Tart mascot	U. hypnotizes you with	U. the next thing you see that is red.
V. The strongest child you know	V. tricks you by getting you to sell your birthright for	V. a small potted plant.
W. A Chinaman	W. chokes you with	W. an HP desktop computer from 1998.
X. Taylor Swift	X. breaks down your door with	X. an Amy Grant CD.
Y. A progressive Catholic priest	Y. roundhouse kicks you with	Y. an essential oils business kit for just $199.99.
Z. Bill Gates	Z. hacks your bunker's security system with	Z. a Sizzler ashtray.

FIELD TRAINING EXERCISES

1. Whom would you like to fight?

   _____

2. Why would you like to fight them?

   _____

3. Is the real reason you want to fight them because they reflect your own weakness
   back at you and you can't bear to face it outright, so you lash out at the people
   around you who are simply trying to do what's best for you?

   _____

4. If you answered no to the last question, then what fight moves would you use
   against them?

   _____

5. If you answered yes to the last last question, then what fight moves would you use
   against them?

   _____

HEADQUARTERS, DEPARTMENT OF THE BABYLON BEE

Chapter 11

Rebuilding Civilization from the Ashes

You've survived the apocalypse. Go you! All those other dummies didn't make it, but because you were smart enough to buy this book for its full retail price of $22.99, you're one of the last survivors on Earth.

It's about this time that you're probably thinking to yourself, "Now what?"

Now you get to do the important work of rebuilding a new civilization from the smoldering wreckage of the old one. How fun! This essential work has been entrusted to you, and you must now dedicate your life to leading humanity into a new golden age of peace and prosperity.

Let's get to work!

PRESERVING WESTERN CIVILIZATION'S KNOWLEDGE

You'll want to make sure that the collected knowledge and wisdom of humanity has been securely stored in an apocalypse-proof facility somewhere. Once the dust settles, you'll need to visit these invaluable time capsules of civilization and extract the most necessary items required for human flourishing.

Here are a few places you'll want to look for all of the most important information:

IMPORTANT CULTURAL CENTERS

The local library
(the section with books about whaling ships)

Kyle Mann's board game collection

Hobby Lobby

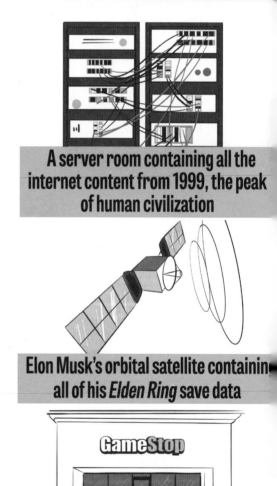

A server room containing all the internet content from 1999, the peak of human civilization

Elon Musk's orbital satellite containing all of his *Elden Ring* save data

GameStop

The Donald Trump Presidential Library

Ark Encounter

The National Archives
(for the treasure map on the back of the Constitution)

Steve
(who has all the baseball stats memorized)

The last Blockbuster Video

Sizzler Steakhouse

MASTERPIECES OF ART AND CIVILIZATION TO SAVE

If you want humanity to enter its new golden age as quickly as possible, you'll need to save all our most important works to be passed down for future generations.

Donald J. Trump ✓
@realDonaldTrump

Despite the constant negative press covfefe

The collected works of Shakespeare

Maybe something by Plato or one of those guys

The recipe for Flamin' Hot Cheetos

Trump's tweets

YouTube clip of the "tears in rain" monologue from *Blade Runner*

Ford plant assembly instructions for the '80 Ford Bronco

MASTERPIECES OF ART AND CIVILIZATION TO SAVE (CONTINUED)

Half-Life 2

A math book
(if you can't find one,
a calculator will work fine)

Biology textbook
(for learning how to make babies
and replenish the human race)

Batman: The Animated Series

Uncle Rick's dry rub secret ingredient

Bluey

WHAT TO SAVE, WHAT TO THROW AWAY

With so many fakes, phonies, spin-offs, and imitations out there, it can be tough to determine which cultural artifacts to keep, and which ones are flaming hot garbage unfit for human civilization. Thankfully, we have a team of seasoned cultural experts here at The Babylon Bee to help you determine what to preserve, and what to leave to the dustbin of the past.

SAVE	THROW AWAY
THE ORIGINAL STAR WARS TRILOGY	ALL THE OTHER STAR WARS MOVIES
THE LORD OF THE RINGS SPECIAL EDITION BLURAY	AMAZON'S *RINGS OF POWER*
DUNE	*DUNE MESSIAH, CHILDREN OF DUNE, GOD EMPEROR OF DUNE, HERETICS OF DUNE, CHAPTERHOUSE: DUNE, HOUSE ATREIDES, HOUSE HARKONNEN, HOUSE CORRINO, THE BUTLERIAN JIHAD, THE MACHINE CRUSADE, THE BATTLE OF CORRIN, HUNTERS OF DUNE, SANDWORMS OF DUNE, PAUL OF DUNE, THE WINDS OF DUNE, SISTERHOOD OF DUNE, MENTATS OF DUNE, NAVIGATORS OF DUNE, DUNE: THE DUKE OF CALADAN, DUNE: THE LADY OF CALADAN, DUNE: THE HEIR OF CALADAN, AND PRINCESS OF DUNE.*

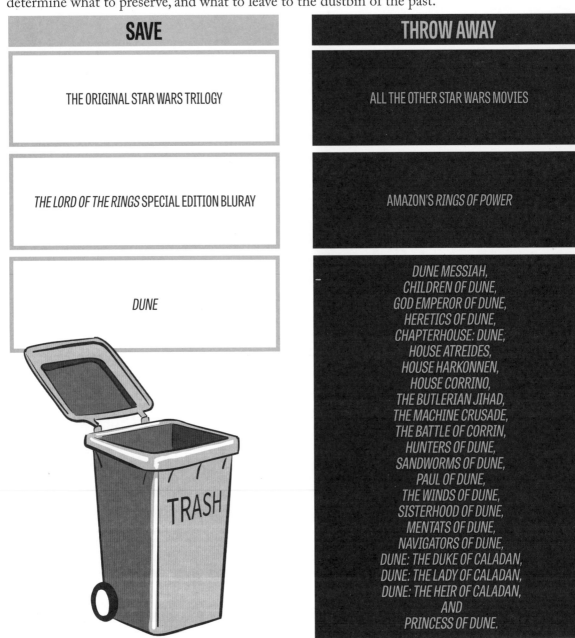

WHAT TO SAVE, WHAT TO THROW AWAY (CONTINUED)

SAVE	THROW AWAY
THE 66 ORIGINAL BOOKS OF THE OLD AND NEW TESTAMENT	THE MESSAGE VERSION
THE BEACH BOYS ALBUM *PET SOUNDS*	ALL OTHER MUSIC—IT ISN'T NEEDED
THE OFFICE SEASONS 1-7	*THE OFFICE* SEASONS 8-9

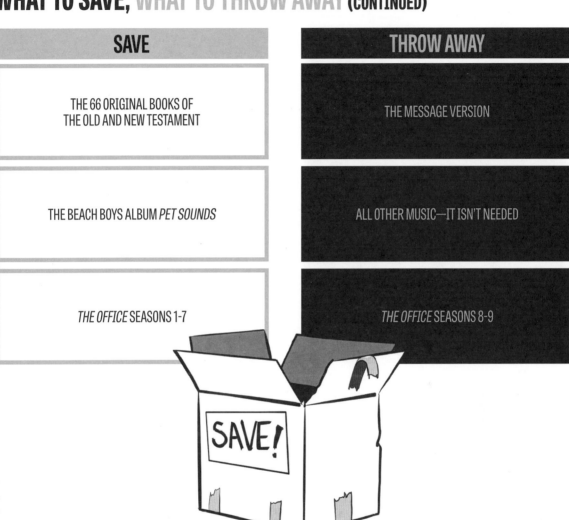

SAVE!

TRAVIS' AVLOGALYPSE
REBUILDING

Scan the QR code to watch Travis rebuild civilization.

https://babylonbee.com/books/
apocalypse/rebuilding

GROWING YOUR OWN FOOD

If you want to see humanity thrive once again, you'll need to reinvent farming. Skip right over the hunter/gatherer phase of civilization and go straight to watching food magically pop out of the ground. So cool!

Things you can plant in your garden:

STEPS FOR BUILDING A POST-APOCALYPTIC FARM

STEP 1

Raid the smoldering wreckage of your local Home Depot or greenhouse and gather all the seeds you can.

Ooo! Cucumbers!

STEP 2

Take the seeds home while fending off swarms of mutants.

It doesn't matter what apocalypse just occurred, there are pretty much always mutants.

STEP 3

Capture the mutants and train them to plow the field and do the planting.

Work smarter, not harder.

STEP 4

Wait a few months.

This is the hardest part.

STEP 5

Time to eat!

Yum!

REPOPULATING THE EARTH

If you're one of the few remaining humans on planet Earth, it is your sacred duty to repopulate it with new humans. Nice. This may seem like a daunting task, but don't worry. We are reproduction experts. Follow this expert advice in order to find a mate and convince them to produce offspring with you.

STEP 1: ATTRACT A MATE

If you want to attract a human partner to repopulate the earth with, you'll first need to make yourself attractive. In order to do this, follow these scientific and gender-specific tips:

MEN

- **WEAR A BRIGHTLY COLORED HEADDRESS AND PERFORM A RITUAL MATING DANCE:** Carefully observe the black-footed albatross for the proper technique.

- **ASK HER IF SHE'S FROM TENNESSEE, BECAUSE SHE'S THE ONLY "10" YOU SEE:** Women really go wild for this line.

- **TELL HER YOU HAVE SOME EXTRA FREEZE-DRIED VENISON IN YOUR APOCALYPSE SHELTER:** It's a date!

- **PROVIDE HER WITH A COMPREHENSIVE LIST OF LOGICAL REASONS WHY SHE SHOULD BE WITH YOU:** Women love logic.

- **BE 6'5", MUSCULAR, AND TAN:** If you're not this, you're unfortunately out of luck.

WOMEN

- **BE A WOMAN:** That's it! You're all set!

STEP 2: TALK TO YOUR NEW MATE

The next step in your human race repopulation project is to talk to the potential mate. Science says this is essential to establishing a relationship, which helps with making human babies. Here are some tips:

MEN

- **ASK HER THINGS ABOUT HER, LIKE HER FAVORITE COLOR:** She'll be impressed by your conversation skills.

- **WHEN SHE TELLS YOU HER FAVORITE COLOR, RESPOND BY TELLING HER YOUR FAVORITE COLOR:** Conversation!

- **TELL HER A DAD JOKE:** It will make her want to turn you into a dad.

- **EXPLAIN TO HER HOW THE FEDERAL RESERVE DESTROYED THE US DOLLAR:** Your vast knowledge will make her swoon.

- **TELL HER YOU'RE DESPERATE:** Her feminine sympathies will kick in and she'll be unable to resist.

WOMEN

- **DON'T TALK:** If you're a woman, talking is completely unnecessary.

STEP 3: TIME TO MAKE THE BABIES

- **ASK YOUR PARENTS HOW THIS WORKS:** This is a Christian book.

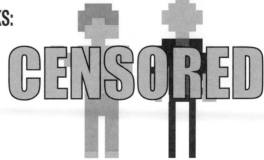

POSSIBLE UTOPIAS TO BUILD

Now that you have a farm and a bunch of kids, it's time to build a new utopia. The cool thing about the world ending is that you get to start from scratch! Now that every kingdom, government, and regime is a smoldering pile of ash, you can build something cooler than anyone ever dreamed of. Are you up to the task? To help your utopia brainstorming session, please consider these totally plausible and achievable utopian visions:

Underwater biodome utopia

Constitutional Republic based on Christian values and natural rights

Land of McDonald's GameCube kiosks

Utopia where everyone gets free ice cream on Thursdays

Floating sky island utopia

Skyline Chili utopia, where everyone eats spaghetti with chili and cheese on top every day

POSSIBLE UTOPIAS TO BUILD (CONTINUED)

Jewtopia

Cool cyberpunk city where everyone has blue hair

Trad-topia where all the women wear aprons and bake sourdough

There you have it, the complete guide to restarting human civilization after the great collapse! There is absolutely nothing else you need to know other than the valuable knowledge we have given you here. Be sure to purchase an extra copy of this book and preserve it in amber so future survivors can rebuild the world if you die.

HAVE FUN!

DEPARTMENT OF THE BABYLON BEE

11 | REBUILDING CIVILIZATION FROM THE ASHES

FIELD TRAINING EXERCISES

1. If you could rebuild civilization with anyone in the world, who would it be? Please write the name of the person below, surrounded by a bunch of cute heart shapes.

   _____

2. Look around you. What is the one thing within arm's reach you would preserve in an apocalypse scenario? Reach out and grab that thing right now, just in case an apocalypse happens while you're reading this.

   _____

3. Draw a blueprint of your farm so you'll know what to plant when the time comes. Then draw a picture of you and your apocalypse mate standing in front of it, surrounded by a bunch of cute heart shapes.

4. Invent a new utopia and write it here:

   _____

5. Now scratch it out so no one steals your cool idea.

   _____

6. The best way to preserve civilization is by storing it in your brain.

Memorize this sonnet:

> Shall I compare thee to a summer's day?
>
> Thou art more lovely and more temperate:
>
> Rough winds do shake the darling buds of May,
>
> And summer's lease hath all too short a date;
>
> Sometime too hot the eye of heaven shines,
>
> And often is his gold complexion dimm'd;
>
> And every fair from fair sometime declines,
>
> By chance or nature's changing course untrimm'd;
>
> But thy eternal summer shall not fade,
>
> Nor lose possession of that fair thou ow'st;
>
> Nor shall death brag thou wander'st in his shade,
>
> When in eternal lines to time thou grow'st:
>
> So long as men can breathe or eyes can see,
>
> So long lives this, and this gives life to thee.
>
> —William Shakespeare

Chapter 12

Glossary of
Apocalypses

As mentioned earlier in the book, The Babylon Bee expended copious sums of money in addition to expired Baskin Robbins gift certificates in the pursuit of pioneering multiversal travel.** It took our research and development team a really long time (at least three weeks, maybe even four), but those nerds actually did it: invented interdimensional travel.

The implications of this breakthrough technology could revolutionize the way our entire world operates. We can now travel to worlds with advanced medicine, world peace, or working McDonald's soft serve machines and share each civilization's society-improving advancements with all other universes, creating a multidimensional age of harmony and prosperity.

What we did instead is even more valuable: we wrote a coffee table book guaranteed to make you lightly chuckle at least once every few pages.

The entirety of our findings could not adequately be detailed in the preceding chapters, so we've written the Chick tract version in the following glossary of multidimensional observations. These scenarios include various, dystopian, utopian, and other just plain weird universes.

TRAVIS' AVLOGALYPSE
THE BEST APOCALYPSE

Scan the QR code
to hear about Travis'
favorite apocalypse.

https://babylonbee.com/books/
apocalypse/best-apocalypse

THE COMPLETE LIST OF
UNIVERSES WE'VE ENCOUNTERED
(NOT COMPREHENSIVE)

THE DAILY WIRE PRESENTS: JEREMY'S NATIONSTATE

The Daily Wire was a conservative news website founded by Jeremy Boreing, Ben Shapiro, and Caleb Robinson. Initially a platform for far-right extremists to spread their hateful ideology, it soon morphed into a media company, producing movies and children's entertainment. Before you could spell "K-L-A-V-A-N," The Daily Wire had also launched a successful line of men's grooming products and also chocolate, for some reason. This was only the beginning.

As more companies proceeded to go woke over the next several decades, The Daily Wire continued to respond in kind, attaching co-CEO and self-styled god-king Jeremy Boreing's name to each item. Jeremy's Razors led to Jeremy's Chocolate. Jeremy's Pendragon Cycle led to Jeremy's Disney. By the time Jeremy's Star Wars came out, normal Star Wars had already organically lost all of its previous fans, who were more than delighted to jump ship to the new version starring Ben Shapiro as Jeremy's Anakin Skywalker. It was no surprise when Boreing finally announced Jeremy's Presidential Bid and upon his election, evoked the Emergency Powers Act of the newly formed Jeremy's Galactic Senate granting him the ability to remain Supreme Chancellor long past his intended election term. Jeremy Boreing was eventually dethroned by his very own clone Jeremy's Jeremy.

THE STARBUCKS EMPIRE

The Starbucks Empire was founded in 1971 in Seattle, WA. Over the next century, it continued to grow as a coffeehouse chain until 2094,[1] at which point it could no longer open any new stores since every building in the world was now a Starbucks. With every building converted and no more landmass available to build new locations, the Starbucks Corporation attempted to reclassify the Pacific Ocean as a foam-capped beverage with Essence of Kelp™. The new drink would only come in one size: Cicciobomba, and was met with mixed reviews. Some tasters of the drink described it as "briny" while others noted that it had a mouthfeel of "really, really bad." With Earth effectively franchised, Starbucks continued outward, spreading across the universe and thereby fulfilling the prophecy of making bucks among the stars. Each new planet discovered was quickly remodeled to add a convenient drive-thru that took longer to order from than if you had simply docked on the planet, picked up your order, and then exited the planet's atmosphere. Even at the height of its power, the Starbucks Empire did not reign entirely unopposed. Lurking in the shadows, a ragtag team of rebels known as The Tea Party simply could not accept the intense notes of toasted caramelization brought out by precisely timed and temperature-controlled roasts performed by handlebar-mustachioed artisans. They instead opted to drink leaf juice like a bunch of self-important aristocrats.

X

In the X dimension, Elon Musk successfully turned X into the universal platform of social media, banking, data storage, orthodontics, gym memberships, tapas restaurants, microbreweries, macrobreweries, and child care (to help look after his 873 children). Every X user was fitted with a Neuralink device with the capability of reading its user's thoughts and sending the best jokes and meme ideas directly to Elon's personal feed. The mandatory Neuralink implant process was detailed in fine print in the terms of service.[2] On the plus side, since X held all of the world's copyrights, trademarks, and tapas restaurants, the Neuralink technology came standard with the ability to trick your brain into making your daily nutritional substance bars taste like piping hot patatas bravas. Yum!

Oh yeah. We also invented time travel. Did we forget to mention that earlier?

It's not his fault you clicked the box.

WWE (AND OTHER WRESTLING FRANCHISES)

In this dimension, various interest groups wrestled for political and social power. Literally. Instead of using boring old methods like talking and diplomacy, they opted for a much sweatier approach. Gross.

THE MCDONALD'S REVOLUTION

In this particular pocket universe, citizens continually voted for minimum wage increases for low-skilled jobs such as that of fast food restaurant employees. After all, everyone deserves to make a living wage. However, the raises didn't stop at $10/hr, nor did they stop at $15/hr. They didn't even stop at $20/hr. These expressionless cashiers with a general disdain for human life continued to receive wage increases until they became the most wealthy humans ever to have lived. With a complete monopoly of the world's fiat currency supply, the rest of the world was left to barter with those Monopoly sweepstakes stickers, which were ironically also controlled by the McDonald's corporation.

DANCE DANCE REVOLUTION

In the early 2000s, inventor and part-time flute salesman Hen Benderson III was at the mall when he noticed an Etnies-clad Chinese teenager playing a rather unique arcade game. The arcade game screen displayed scrolling arrows that players were to match with rhythmic stomping upon corresponding sensor pads below their feet. This game was called *Dance Dance Revolution.* As he witnessed the joy this lanky wallet chain–wearing hooligan experienced while "dancing," an ingenious idea came to mind. What if he installed these machines on every street corner of America so that everyday citizens could enjoy a quick game while waiting for the crosswalk? The energy produced by the stomping motion could be harnessed to provide sustainable power to the general population at zero cost to the taxpayer. He proposed this plan to the US government and was given the go-ahead to install 100 machines apiece in several major US cities. What he did not foresee was that all of these machines being used at once could (and did) create a seismic event that eventually ruptured the earth's crust and caused molten lava to surface, destroying the eastern seaboard and also a single Long John Silver's franchise in Oceanside, CA. The world was never the same again.

WOMBAT WORLD

There exists in the multiverse a world where humans have all died out and wombats have become apex predators, selfishly depleting all natural resources and eating all other animals without remorse. Not much else is known about this dimension since Travis was immediately eaten by wombats as soon as he entered this dimension. The Travis that returned to report back for this book was actually an elite member of a breed of shapeshifting wombatkin who assumed a Travis-like shape in order to plant the seeds of an interdimensional takeover.

KAIJU

This dimension closely mirrored that of our own up until 1954 when an eldritch beast emerged from the Pacific Ocean and decimated several islands off the coast of Montana. The beast was described by onlookers as "meh" and "What that thing is?" After a few days of casual rampaging, the beast returned to the sea, but left humanity with this ominous warning, "Follow your dreams, kids!" The image above is an artist's depiction of the creature as published in a Montana newspaper in 1954.

THE GHOST DIMENSION

The world hit its total death capacity, causing ghosts to overlap each other with no elbow room whatsoever. Everything was haunted, nothing was safe. But, with too many ghosts, the spirits began to haunt each other, creating a poltergeist paradox. This caused a breakdown in the very fabric of reality, leading to the complete collapse of all matter in the universe. Technically, the dimension still exists, but it's a bunch of ghosts floating in an empty void, doing nothing.

THE ONE WHERE ALL THE WOMEN DISAPPEAR

All the women disappeared for some reason. The men, desperate for companionship, traveled through a dimensional portal to try and find the women. However, when they traveled through the one-time-use portal to the woman universe, they found that all the women had left to try to find the man universe.

THE ONE WHERE ALL THE MEN DISAPPEAR

All the men disappeared for some reason. The women, desperate for companionship, traveled through a dimensional portal to try and find the men. However, when they traveled through the one-time-use portal to the man universe, they found that all the men had left to try to find the woman universe. This major shifting event became known as The Ol' Switcheroo, a term coined by historian and known hairdresser Javius Flosephus.

THE RETURN OF CIRCUIT CITY

"Welcome to Circuit City, where everything's state of the art." These are the words of the late Bob Circuit who founded the popular Circuit City electronics store and lifestyle brand. Despite going out of business in our universe, Circuit City is thriving in at least 78% of all other known universes. In many dimensions, Circuit City is also a popular name given to baby boys and sometimes even girls. Many of these other universes are aware of the brand's multidimensional presence and have formed a Coalition of Circuit City Universes[3] governed by an elected board of prophets known as the Council of Circuit City. The Council has collectively prophesied that "The Reign of Circuit City has only just begun," and that in 30 years time, Circuit City will return to our dimension as both a lifestyle brand and also a more fair and equitable form of government we can all rely on.

SUN GOES SUPERNOVA

The sun exploded. Ouch.

HAROLD BECOMES KING

In this universe, Harold becomes king.

---

[3] The Council meets in the capital city known as Circuit City City.

CORE IMPLOSION

"Nathan" found a switch below the diamond mines of Raktu Landra that he was sure would turn the lights on. However, it caused the earth's core to implode. The origins of the switch are unknown, and no one survived the event to investigate further. Hilary Swank did not survive. Sadly, Joseph Gordon-Levitt did.

THE GREAT IKEA LABYRINTH

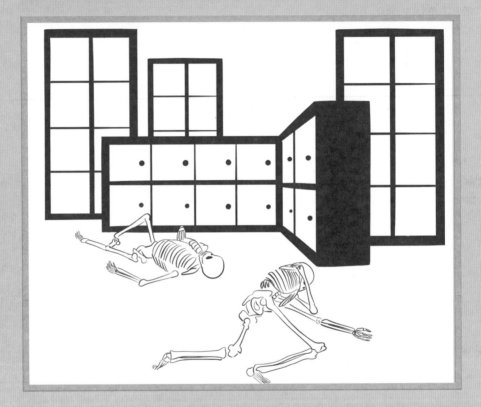

It all started with the great deals on meatballs and lingonberry sauce. Once they got you through those wide double doors, leaving was not an option. While an exit to the furniture maze was theorized to exist, others claimed the idea of an exit was a myth told to the Ikean people to offer false hope and keep them in a state of peace. Ikean citizens were forced to live out the rest of their days endlessly wandering past KALLAX shelving and the timelessly classic ELVARLI wardrobe storage and organization system. People lived and died within those warehouse walls, but strangely, no bodies were ever seen being removed from the premises. Conversely, no meatballs were ever seen delivered into the stores.

DISNEY'S HOUSE OF MOUSE

In a move nobody didn't see coming, the Disney Corporation bought the entire world. It started with Pixar, Star Wars, Marvel, and every other beloved intellectual property, but eventually, Disney accumulated enough money to purchase the entire world economy and every world leader and government. This happened during President Donald Trump's 6th term, right after the president jailed former Florida Governor Ron DeSantis for "eating pudding the wrong way." With DeSantis safely tucked behind bars, the mouse was freed from his trap and could now purchase anything and make it retroactively gay. Bluey? Gay. Mr. Rogers? Gay. The Babylon Bee? Gay. Barack Obama? Unchanged.

JERRY'S ARCADE UNIVERSE

On September 14th of 1997, Jerry Brigham from Parkville, Missouri fulfilled his lifelong dream of opening an arcade to help keep kids off the streets and out of trouble. On opening day, neighborhood children with parents in tow and the occasional skiball-loving adult lined up for the grand opening of Jerry's Arcade Universe. The local teens loved having a place to hang out after school and play a few games of *Turtles in Time* or foosball even though the red team had the clear advantage since the blue team had a player with his legs broken off. During hot summer days, kids would put a quarter in the air hockey table and then lay on top of it as the air rushed up from the tiny holes in its surface. Jerry's younger brother Greg made the best nachos within a 50-mile radius, and sold them for only $1.00, so even the ugly poor kids could enjoy the gooey cheese sauce made from real cheese and not the canned stuff. When Jerry eventually passed away in 2022, his will revealed that the beloved establishment would be inherited by "whoever has the highest score on the *Ms. Pac-Man* machine." That score was held by local resident Stacy Childers[4] who could not be reached for comment.

[^] It was a girl, cause only girls play *Ms. Pac Man*.

NORTH KOREA

In this pocket dimension, Glorious Leader Kim Jong Un realized all he had to do to conquer the already flailing Western world was to have his troops shout proper pronouns at enemy soldiers. The soy-fed US troops and their limp wrists didn't stand a chance.

THE SECRET OF MAGNETS

The secret behind how magnets work was discovered in this universe. Turns out there are tiny creatures living inside of all magnets playing tug of war with warring colonies. The threads they pull are so tiny, they do not register to the human eye. As the magnets get closer to each other, the colonies are able to see the warring tribe and pull harder and harder, drawing the magnets together. In the universe that discovered this phenomenon, the magnet people did not appreciate humans observing them and formed an alliance against humanity. They destroyed almost all of human society with their magnetic powers, pulling down skyscrapers, and eventually pulling the moon into the surface of the earth.

THE GUN-CONTROLLED PARADISE

This is not an apocalypse world, but instead a utopia in which the free people of the world elected Alexandria Ocasio-Cortez Supreme Leader, and her first act in power was to make guns illegal. Once guns were made illegal, all the criminals in the world turned in their weaponry and denounced their former ways. All the good guys welcomed all the bad guys back into society and threw a pizza party to commemorate the occasion. That celebration marked the date of the most popular holiday, known from that point on as All-the-Bad-Guys-Are-Good-Now Day. All it took was a little common-sense gun control.

THE FROGZONE

Words cannot describe the horrors witnessed in this world. Every time we attempt to describe this universe, we fall into fits of apoplectic frenzy and require weeks of intense therapy before we are able to even speak another word or maintain eye contact with other human beings. Even the act of typing these words out has caused irreparable PTSD for which healing may never come. The Frogzone... Do not venture there. DO NOT VENTURE THERE.

NERF WARS

Foam mayhem. Non-lethal violence. Fast-moving objects that could possibly hurt if they hit you directly in the eye. These are a few concepts that describe the unending Nerf Wars in this distant universe. In the 1990s, Parker Brothers expanded their popular Nerf foam ball line to include the very first Nerf foam dart blaster along with a new motto, "It's Nerf or Nothin'!" Many people took that idea too literally and soon formed Nerf gangs that overthrew all world governments and eventually the world. Nerf turf wars were kinda weird, cause nobody ever actually got hurt, but they still happened, albeit very ineffectively.

CHRISTOPHER NOLAN'S CONFUSION OF THE LANGUAGES

The early 21st century led to a second "confusion of the languages" event when director Christopher Nolan opted to release a film shot entirely underwater with 3D IMAX cameras and played in reverse order. Every character spoke through a satellite phone with a weak signal to the past, reporting on the destruction of Atlantis while wearing scuba gear. Viewers left the theater stunned, unable to speak, but quite sure they would think the movie was brilliant if they had a chance to watch it at least three more times. Unfortunately, the world shut down shortly thereafter, and its population gradually died off, unable to convey even the simplest ideas to their friends and family.

VALVE RELEASES *HALF-LIFE 3*

In the year 3434.2, under the leadership of Gabe Newell Jr. Jr. Jr. Jr. Jr. Jr. Jr. Esq., Valve Software (then known as Microsoft Activision Blizzard Valve Bethesda) released *Half-Life 3*. Early development of the title was initially halted by Gabe Newell Prime (hereby reckoned as GNP) over fear that its eventual release would bring about the end of the world due to the creation and subsequent collapse of a theoretical "joy singularity." However, his writings were lost to time (misplaced under unreleased copies of *Left 4 Dead 3* and *Portal 3*) and development was eventually completed. Upon release, the game received a 9.7 review from IGN just before the world collapsed in on itself, killing trillions.

THE REMAINING 13,999,975 OTHER APOCALYPTIC UNIVERSES

The rest of the apocalyptic worlds Travis visited are all pretty boring, and our publisher informed us that it would be slightly out of our budget to put the rest of them to paper.

We hope this completely comprehensive, abridged list of the end times scenarios of all possible universes has been helpful. Have you encountered a different apocalypse? Let us know by writing it down on the following page, taking a picture, going to get that picture developed at the pharmacy, and then faxing that picture to us.

[YOUR OWN ENTRY]

_____

_____

_____

_____

_____

_____

_____

_____

_____

_____

_____

_____

_____

_____

_____

_____

_____

_____

_____

_____

_____

_____

_____

_____

Afterword

A
Final Word

Well, you've made it. You've survived the apocalypse. You may have even started rebuilding civilization, but we still have a long road ahead of us. It's gonna take a lot of work. You might even have to put some hours in on nights and weekends. You probably won't even make minimum wage. That really sucks, but it is necessary. It's necessary to take humanity forward into the next phase, no matter what life has to throw at us next. So thank you. You're doing a good job, buddy.

ABOUT THE AUTHORS

Kyle Mann is the editor-in-chief of The Babylon Bee and co-author of *How to Be a Perfect Christian*, *The Sacred Texts of The Babylon Bee*, *The Babylon Bee Guide* series, and *The Postmodern Pilgrim's Progress*. He lives in the greater San Diego region with his wife, Destiny, and their three boys, Emmett, Samuel, and Calvin. They may or may not have a survival bunker under their house.

Joel Berry is the managing editor of The Babylon Bee, co-author of *The Babylon Bee Guide to Wokeness*, *The Postmodern Pilgrim's Progress*, *The Babylon Bee Guide to Democracy*, and *The Babylon Bee Guide to Gender*. He is also a columnist, a former worship leader, and a public speaker. He lives with his wife and six kids in Ohio.

Brandon Toy was the director of video production at The Babylon Bee until the woke mind virus wiped out 90% of human civilization and all remaining conservatives were forced into hiding. He survives in his Hobbit-hole themed bunker with his wife Amy and four cats Petra, Fable, Lychee, & Library who are trained to retrieve crucial survival supplies such as a fuzzy pink heart that's been chewed on so much that the stuffing is coming out of it.

ABOUT THE ARTISTS

Bettina La Savio is the creative designer for The Babylon Bee. She lives in SoCal with her two daughters and psychotic cats Sushi and Jelly Bean who make her house look like the apocalypse has already hit. She did not read this book in time to prepare for the actual apocalypse and has since been eaten by wombats.

Travis Woodside is a staff writer at The Babylon Bee and doomsday enthusiast. His hobbies include playing movies, video games, and long walks on the beach. He lives in southern California with his wife and two daughters. It is his dream to one day own and manage his own Sizzler restaurant.

Bryan Ming is the project and operations manager at The Babylon Bee. He's not paid to be funny, he just does it for free.

SPECIAL THANKS

Dan Coats   **Kristin Oren**

ACKNOWLEDGMENTS

Kyle would like to thank his wife, Destiny, who is eternally patient and longsuffering as he tries out Babylon Bee jokes on her. He laughs. She does not. She still loves him. Wow—true love! He also would like to thank his three boys, Emmett, Samuel, and Calvin, for helping him keep his sanity. And the rest of his family and friends are pretty cool too.

Joel would like to thank Seth Dillon, Dan Dillon, and Kyle Mann for building the Bee and giving him the greatest job in the world, his gorgeous wife Kelsey who fills his home with beautiful things and works hard to keep his adorable kids out of his office while he's writing, and his sovereign, faithful, and all-wise Creator.

Brandon would like to first and foremost thank God for the grace, love, and acceptance he doesn't deserve; His wife Amy for being the literal and objectively best person in the world, Matt Walsh for sharing his exact birthdate, Seth and Dan Dillon for letting him tell jokes for money, Thomas Sowell, Ken Sugimori, Nathan Fielder, Jordan Peterson, and of course Steve from Fruitport, Michigan.

Bettina would like to thank God for giving her the weirdest, most fun job she's ever had. Also the Bee Boys for subjecting her to random nerdy trivia she has no interest in knowing. She's grateful to her kiddos Lala and Zoe-Zoe for their enthusiastic participation in modeling for various drawings and willingness to be dragged into the office.

Travis would like to thank his help meet, Laura, who drew the bicep for an alien depicted in this book. His children are also deserving of praise for making the work less depressing by peering over his shoulder and laughing at all the stick figures he made. Third of all, God comes first.

Bryan would like to thank God for His increasing and unceasing faithfulness and provision. He is also thankful for his wife, who supports him in all of his endeavors, despite all of his imperfections.

And all of us at The Babylon Bee would like to thank the heroes who fought bravely (but unsuccessfully) to save Western civilization before its untimely demise:

Our CEO Seth Dillon who signs our paychecks, Elon Musk, Carman, every housewife in the nation who's quietly raising her kids and doesn't even post it to Instagram, Sizzler steakhouses, well-known Canadian man Dr. Jordan B. Peterson, Krispy Kreme, Inc., J.R.R. Tolkien, Skip-It by Tiger Electronics, Gary Gygax, Old Spice, Waffle House, New Balance sneakers, every Christian ska band, Montell Jordan, writer of the 1995 hit R&B single "This Is How We Do It," people who still wear a full suit and tie to baseball games, and Greg.

This book is dedicated to
the memory of Travis—

always jumping into one more dimension,
hoping that the next time he jumps,
it will be the jump home.